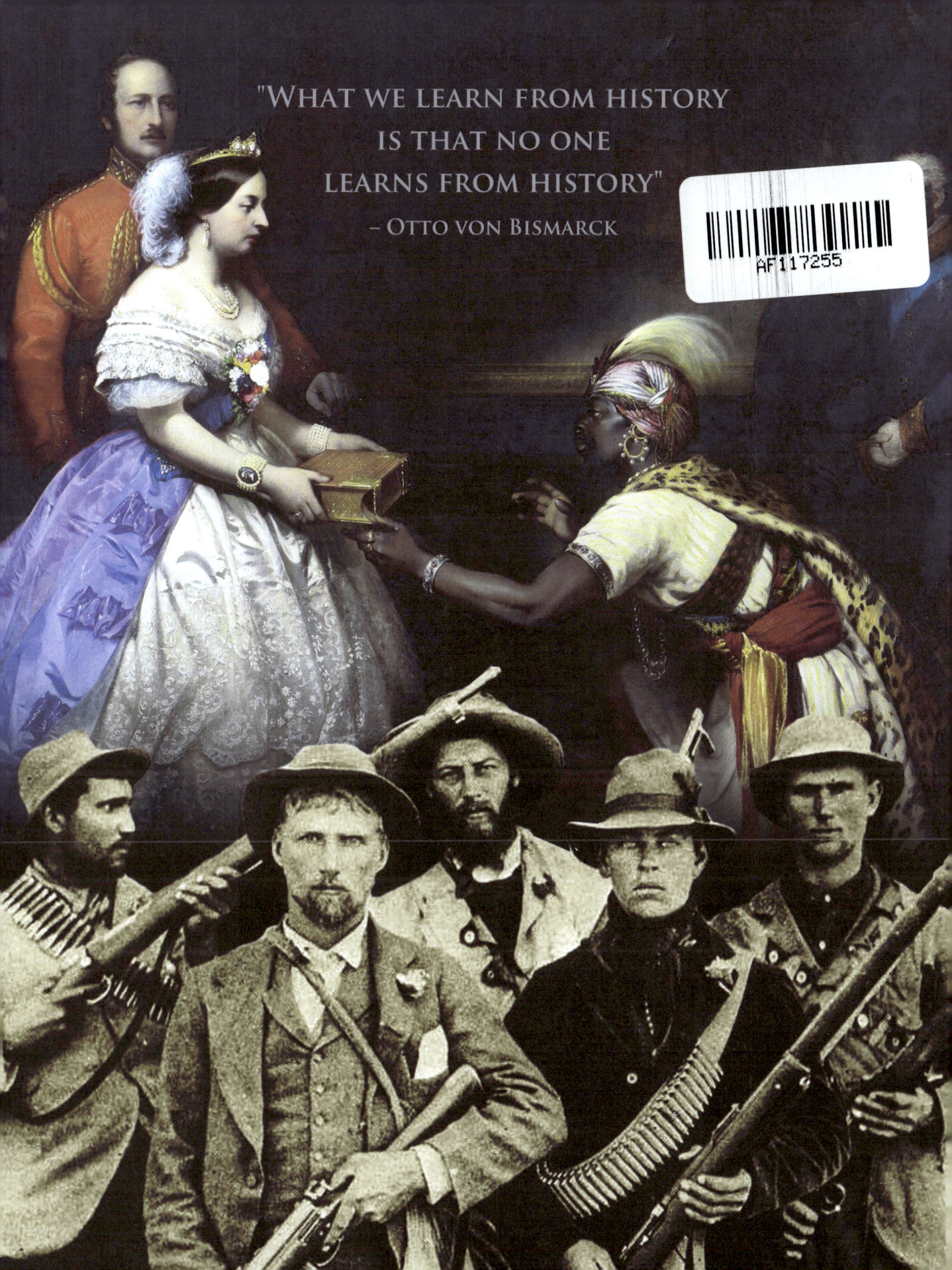

"What we learn from history is that no one learns from history"
– Otto von Bismarck

QUEEN VICTORIA
1819 – 1901

English King William IV had no kids eligible to inherit the throne. Actually, he had 10 kids – all born before he became king. But their mom was an actress, William's girlfriend, so they were 'illegitimate' children, born to an unmarried couple. Plus, their mom was a 'commoner,' not an aristocrat, not a royal. As a result, King William's niece, Princess Alexandrina Victoria, named after her godfather, Russian Emperor Alexander I, was raised to be the queen. Victoria's dad died when she was a baby. Her mom taught her to save money, work for charity projects and be "self-reliant and brave." To train her to perform public duties, Victoria's mom took her daughter on trips to military forts, arsenals, lighthouses, and battleships. The royal guests presented new *colors* (flags) to garrisons and crews, and were treated to dinners. Victoria was also kept away from King William's court, because the king – though warm and witty – had a habit of swearing "like a sailor." Actually, he was a sailor! In his youth he had served in the Royal Navy. His nickname was the 'Sailor King.'

Victoria was a good writer, a talented artist, and had many other gifts, but it was her royal blood that determined her future. When King William died in 1837, 18-year-old Victoria was awakened in her mom's bedroom (she was afraid to sleep alone).

Below: The earliest photograph of Queen Victoria, 1844; Victoria at age 4
Right: Young Victoria's portrait by Franz Xaver Winterhalter

The Archbishop of Canterbury (the leader of the Church of England) kneeled in front of her and handed her the certificate of the king's death. England was a constitutional monarchy, so Victoria's first speech of her reign – before the Privy Council (royal advisors) – included the words, "I have learned from infancy to respect and love the Constitution of my native country." She read the speech with the confidence and dignity that extinguished the sneers of the skeptical council members. Victoria was proclaimed queen standing by the open window of the Privy Council Chamber. Vast crowds on the square below shouted "God save the Queen!" Cannons fired salutes, the bands played the national anthem, and Victoria burst into tears.

Next, Victoria had to sit through another Privy Council meeting and then stand at the reception for bishops and judges. Her conduct projected authority and grace "as if she had done nothing else all her life." Once the reception was over she slowly walked out of the room looking as regal as could be...However, the reception room had glass doors, so the guests were stunned when, as the doors closed, they could see the queen pull up her skirt and dash down the hall running, relieved that the torture was over! Then there was the coronation and *Vivat Regina!* ('Long live the Queen' in Latin) sung by every choir in London, and then... the 64-year-long reign of Queen Victoria began.

"Victoria learns about King William's death" by Henry Tanworth Wells; Right: Victoria's self-portrait

Describing the early Victorian era, British historian M.B.Synge, wrote: "It was a very different Britain at that time...there were few books to read, and these were expensive. There were no free libraries...Baths were not considered necessary. Eton [famous boarding school] boys had one bath a term, and that was the night before they returned home for the holidays! Beer was the universal drink for rich and poor. There was no five o'clock tea, because tea was expensive. There was no British Empire. Australia was a convict colony, South Africa a little territory around the Cape of Good Hope, New Zealand was inhabited by natives only. Few people thought much of these scattered possessions, some did not even know where they lay on the map."

However, as Victoria became queen, the world around her was going through a massive transformation. This was the high point of the industrial revolution (1760-1840). The first passenger trains appeared in England, and steam-engine ships started regular voyages between England and New York City, taking 'only' 2 weeks to cross the Atlantic. The English postal service introduced cheap postage stamps, so sending letters and packages by mail became affordable to all. The electric telegraph opened for use in 1842 offering instant communication between cities. All of a sudden the faraway colonies of Europe seemed closer and easier to reach. The legends of colonial resources promised instant wealth. And so, the new round of empire building began, with its inevitable consequence – brutal wars.

Every day young Queen Victoria spent 4-5 hours with the British Prime Minister Lord Melbourne (Melbourne, Australia, was named in his honor in 1837). Melbourne trained her in world politics and government affairs. Every day she was handed documents to sign, and she read every single one, even when Melbourne asked for her signature with the words, "Your Majesty, there is no need to examine this paper...it's of no special importance." Victoria was an enthusiastic student, but there were many things Melbourne and her other ministers and advisors preferred not to inform her about – at least not in detail. Things like...the British invasion of Afghanistan.

The British East India Company had seized and colonized large portions of India. With the permission of the British government, it ruled India, and now it had its eyes on Afghanistan. Concerned about Russian influence on the Afghan ruler, Dost Mohammad, the *East India Company* joined forces with the British government to overthrow him. In December 1838 the invasion force of 21,000 British and Indian troops and 38,000 'camp followers' (servants, vendors, food providers) on 30,000 camels entered Afghanistan and took Kabul. This was the beginning of the *First Anglo-Afghan War* (1839-1842).

Another war, unleashed by Lord Melbourne and the East India Company in 1839, was the ***First Opium War*** with China. Britain's most profitable trade of the 19th century was the import of ***opium*** (a drug made from poppy plants) into China, where opium was banned. The East India Company sold opium in China illegally, and used the money it made to pay for Chinese tea it imported to Britain. When the Chinese government seized the stock of illegal opium and threatened opium sellers with the death penalty, the British government declared that China must respect the 'principles of free trade' and change its opium law. The British navy was promptly sent to the coast of China to 'help' it 'change its attitude.'

Meanwhile Victoria moved into Buckingham Palace – the first British monarch to make it her residence. But there was a problem. In 1839 Victoria quarreled with her mom over some court intrigues. However, custom required that as an unmarried woman she should live with her mother, even though she was a queen. Lord Melbourne advised Victoria to get married. She called his idea a "shocking alternative," but a few months later she fell in love with her cousin, German prince Albert of Saxe-Coburg and Gotha. Victoria wrote in her diary: "At half past twelve I sent for Albert. He came to my room where I was alone. After a few minutes I said to him that I thought he must be aware why I wished him to come, and that it would make me very happy if he would consent to what I wished – that he should marry me... I told him I was quite unworthy of him. He said he would be very happy to spend his life with me." Four months later they were married. Victoria and Albert's marriage was happy and lasted 21 years until his death. Interesting fact: Victoria's white wedding dress started the tradition of European brides wearing white. Until then wedding dresses had come in all colors.

"Queen Victoria's Family" by Franz Xaver Winterhalter

To get away from Victoria's mom, Victoria and Albert moved into Windsor Castle, and found themselves all alone in a dusty ancient space falling apart before their eyes. The 3 officials who were supposed to run the royal household were the Lord Steward, the Lord Chamberlain, and the Master of the Horse, but, over the centuries, these positions became honorary titles given to men of high rank. None of them was around. The royals were lucky when there was at least one servant in the palace. On most days there was none. When the Prime Minister of France stayed as a guest at Windsor, it took him over an hour to find his bedroom. A boy from a nearby village wandered into the castle – through the doors nobody guarded – and was found sleeping under a sofa. The worker who brought wood for the fireplace refused to light the fire because his department didn't have that responsibility. Replacing a broken window glass required the signatures of 4 managers nowhere to be found. Tired of fighting the clumsy outdated system that governed the life of the royal family, Victoria and Albert bought themselves a house on the Isle of Wight – off the south coast of England, in the English Channel.

In 1840 Victoria and Albert had the first of their 9 children, Victoria. "This day last year I was an unmarried girl," wrote Victoria in her diary, "and this year I have an angelic husband, and a dear little girl five weeks old...It seems like a dream to have a child." It was a happy year for the royal family, and Prince Albert agreed with Lord Melbourne that the queen didn't need to hear every single bit of news that came from overseas. Some news was good – the empire kept growing. The British were winning the First Opium War. As a result of the peace treaty, the Chinese island of Hong Kong would become a British colony. Also, the New Zealand Colonization Company was formed. It started sending colonists to settle in New Zealand, and in 1840 native Maori chiefs gave up their sovereignty under the Treaty of Waitangi. New Zealand was now a British colony as well.

But Afghanistan was a disaster. And this was only the *First* Anglo-Afghan War...The son of Dost Mohammad, Akbar Khan, raised an army of rebels and marched on Kabul. Commander of the British garrison in Kabul arranged peace talks with Akbar Khan, but in the middle of negotiation Akbar Khan shot him. His body was dragged through the streets of Kabul and displayed in the bazaar. The British garrison – 4,500 troops and 12,000 servants and soldiers' families – left Kabul for Jalalabad, but as they were making their way through the Khyber Pass (a mountain pass in present-day Pakistan), they were attacked by 30,000 Afghan rebels. A small number of servants, women, and children were taken prisoner. Everybody else was killed, except six British officers who managed to escape on horseback. Out of the six, however, only one made it to Jalalabad.

Above: "The Last Stand in Khyber Pass" by William Barnes Wollen
Below: "The remnant of an Army – Jalalabad" by Elizabeth Southerden Thompson, Lady Butler

In addition, yet another war was brewing... this time in South Africa, the "Garden Colony" – a beautiful well-watered land where English colonists settled around the Cape of Good Hope, side-by-side with Dutch farmers called the **Boers**. While the English had abolished slavery, the Dutch continued to use slave labor. They defeated the local **Zulu** tribes and were actively colonizing the areas called **Natal** and **Transvaal**. When Boers declared Natal a republic in 1842, Queen Victoria's government sent troops to drive the Boers out of Natal – to Transvaal.

While being kept at a distance from the foreign dealings of her government, Victoria was not isolated from the life of common citizens. She was aware of the poverty in the city streets and the intolerable work conditions in the coal mines. One of the social causes she paid special attention to was child labor. All the heating in Britain was provided by wood- and coal-burning fireplaces, and all the chimneys were cleaned by boys, mostly under 8 years old. Little 'chimney sweepers' were pushed into the chimneys, and if they didn't work fast enough, their boss stuck lighted straw into the chimney so that fire and sparks would force the child to move faster up the chimney. Many kids died   suffocated by the soot, or broke bones falling down chimneys.

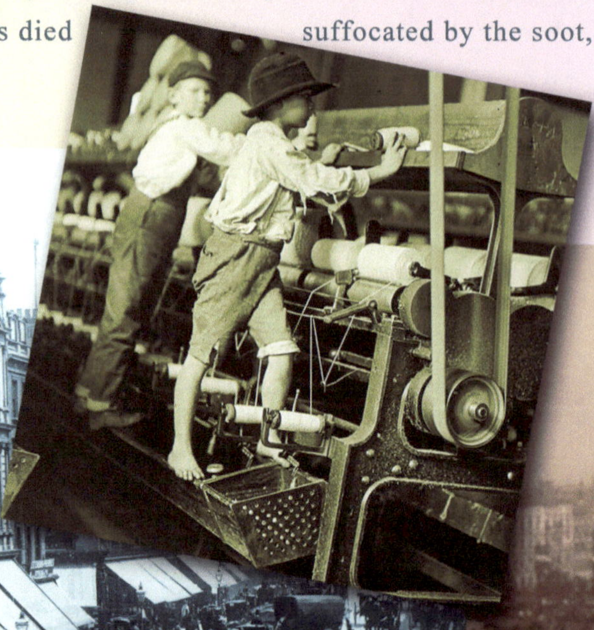

Transvaal Boer, 19th-century photo

Kid factory workers; a little chimney sweeper; the streets of London - 19th-century photos

With the encouragement of Queen Victoria, in 1840 the British Parliament passed an act forbidding kids under 10 from working in chimneys. Another problem was child employment at factories and in coal mines. Kids as young as 4 years old worked dawn to sunset at factories producing buttons, tobacco, glass – all sorts of common goods. In coal mines 8-year-olds crawled on their knees and elbows along narrow coal mine passages, pulling coal-loaded carts strapped to their waists with a chain, while 4-year-olds sat in total darkness 12 hours at a time opening and closing the ventilation doors of the mine. Both employers and parents considered this normal. Kids were paid very little, but this money kept many families from starvation. Finally, in 1845 Britain banned any employment of children under 8, and 2 years later the *Ten Hours Bill* was passed limiting the workday to 10 hours. Queen Victoria actively promoted the adoption of all these new laws.

Meanwhile a revolutionary wave was rising in Europe. The poverty of the urban population and the middle class' demand for more rights produced the ideas of *liberalism* and *socialism*. In London many viewed the royal family as a symbol of social injustice. In 1840, while Queen Victoria was pregnant with her first baby, an 18-year-old Englishman, Edward Oxford, shot a pistol at the queen as she was riding in an open-top carriage. He was seized by the police and tried for high treason, but found not guilty. The court declared him insane and sent him to a mental asylum. Later his sentence was replaced with the so-called *transportation* – exile of convicted criminals to British colonies, mostly Australia. Oxford was the first of 7 men who tried to assassinate Queen Victoria. Two more assassination attempts happened 2 years later. One of the assassins was sentenced to death, but his sentence was also replaced with the 'transportation for life.' The other was declared mentally ill and received an 18-month jail term. In 1845, in Ireland, the potato crop failed, and the *Great Famine* killed over a million Irish over 4 years. Another million emigrated to the United States and British colonies. In Ireland, Victoria was nicknamed "The Famine Queen," and in 1849 an unemployed Irishman committed another failed assassination attempt.

Edward Oxford shoots at Queen Victoria

Liberalism and Socialism

Liberalism is a political philosophy defending civil liberties (such as freedom of speech and religion), equality of citizens' rights and opportunities, democracy, and freedom to start and run any business. The traditional understanding of liberalism does not include **equity** *– equality of results or outcome. Example: equality of opportunity vs equality of results (= equity) in job search.*
Equality of opportunity: *All citizens have equal access to employment, but their chance of being hired, the type of job they can get, and their salaries depend on individual citizens' talents, education, commitment, and so on. Some do better and some do worse.*
Equality of results: *Any citizen should be able to get hired for a job, whether they are the best candidate for it or not. Salaries should be equal, whether the workers are talented and hard-working or not.*
Equity is a feature of socialism, the social-economic system where all enterprises (plants, factories, all businesses) belong not to individual business owners or companies, but to the state, and the state employs everyone equally and pays equal salaries to everyone irrespective of their abilities and productivity.

In February of 1848 a revolution erupted in France. French King Louis Philippe lost his throne, fled to England, and the French **Second Republic** was established. The anti-monarchy rebellions spread to Italy, Germany and France. Fearing an uprising in London, Queen Victoria's family moved permanently to the Isle of Wight. In their new home the royal family lived a much simpler lifestyle than in London. Victoria's kids were taught cooking and carpentry. Each kid had a vegetable garden and sold the vegetables to the royal kitchen at market price. The boys were required to spend 7 hours a day in school. All Victoria's kids gained fluency in English, German, and French. Both Victoria and Albert taught their kids respect. When Victoria overheard her oldest daughter, Vicky, address their family doctor as "Brown" (not "Doctor Brown"), she told her, "If you do this again, I'll send you to bed." The next morning, Vicky greeted Dr.Brown, "Good morning, Brown!..." And added, "And good night, because I am going to bed!" Whenever Prince Albert crossed the London Bridge, the bridge keeper saluted him and Albert returned the salute. One day he was crossing the bridge with his oldest son. The bridge keeper saluted, Albert returned the salute, but his son didn't. Albert stopped their carriage and made his son walk back and salute the bridge keeper. The royal family released postcards with the photos of their everyday life, and they sold in huge numbers.

*The Osborne House,
Victoria's home on the Isle of Wight*

"We, women, are not made for governing," wrote Victoria, "and if we are good women, we must dislike these masculine occupations." So Victoria chose to spend more and more time with her family, traveling back to London only for state ceremonies. One grand celebration was held at Buckingham Palace in honor of the 250th anniversary of the East India Company. In 1849 the East India Company defeated the **Sikh Empire**, and captured **Punjab**. All the property of its ruler, the Maharajah of Lahore, was confiscated by the British as compensation for war expenses, including the legendary **Koh-i-noor** diamond, one of the largest cut diamonds in the world (105.6 carats = 21.12 g). Koh-i-noor means "Mountain of Light" in Persian and Hindi/Urdu. It was brought from Punjab to Buckingham Palace and presented to Queen Victoria by officials of the East India Company as a symbol of British rule over India.

Then, in 1854, the **Crimean War** broke out. The new ruler of France, Napoleon III (a nephew of Napoleon Bonaparte), decided to return France to its former greatness. His first move was to "poke the Russian bear." He demanded that Catholic France get undivided authority over the Christian population of Palestine which was under the rule of the **Turkish Ottoman Empire**. Russian Tsar Nicholas I viewed this as an infringement on the rights of Eastern Orthodox Christians in Palestine. However, Napoleon III bribed the Ottoman Sultan, and convinced England to join the anti-Russian alliance. In a show of force, Russian troops marched into the Turkish provinces of Moldavia and Wallachia (present-day Moldova and Romania), but didn't succeed and ended up withdrawing. War could have been prevented, but British and French newspapers raised such a tsunami of anti-Russian propaganda, that the public in both countries demanded war against Russia.

So in 1854 Queen Victoria's government joined forces with the French to attack the Russian port of Sevastopol in **Crimea**, a large peninsula in the Black Sea. Crimea had been a province of Russia since 1783 when the troops of Russian Tsarina Catherine the Great defeated the Ottoman Empire. The first British regiments departing for Crimea marched through the courtyard of Buckingham Palace. Victoria stood on the balcony waving goodbye. Then she rushed to the Isle of Wight to see off the British Navy leaving for the war.

After 2 years of fighting, Russia was losing the Crimean War. Even though they kept Crimea, their naval base in Sevastopol and the Russian Black Sea fleet were destroyed. However, in England and France the public was in shock at the massive losses suffered by French and British troops, with no visible gains. In England they were especially shaken by the famous **Charge of the Light Brigade** at the **Battle of Balaclava** (a suburb of Sevastopol).

The **Light Brigade** was a unit of British cavalry ordered to attack a Russian artillery battery. The assault was conducted head on, under Russian fire, on October 25, 1854. Most of the British cavalry men perished or were taken prisoner. The insanity of the order and the suicidal bravery of the British left the Russians puzzled. Russian newspapers suggested that maybe the attackers were all drunk. A French general who witnessed the attack said words that became famous: "It was magnificent, but it wasn't war." Indeed, it looked more like a slaughter.

Above: Charge of the Light Brigade; Below: Fighting at the Russian artillery positions

A month and a half later, the English poet, Lord Tennyson, published his poem *The Charge of the Light Brigade*.

Half a league, half a league,
Half a league onward,
All in the valley of Death
Rode the six hundred.
"Forward, the Light Brigade!
Charge for the guns!" he said.
Into the valley of Death
Rode the six hundred.

"Forward, the Light Brigade!"
Was there a man dismayed?
Not though the soldier knew
Someone had blundered.
Theirs not to make reply,
Theirs not to reason why,
Theirs but to do and die.
Into the valley of Death
Rode the six hundred.

The Victoria Cross (VC), the highest British military decoration, established by Queen Victoria

The queen and her daughters sewed and knit for the army, raised money for soldiers' families, and delivered medals to wounded soldiers at hospitals, but neither Victoria, nor the British public knew what the war was like until – right in the middle of the war – the profession of newspaper *correspondent* was born. A British military doctor on the frontlines of the Crimean War started sending letters to **the London Times**. He reported about the horrors of war, and also about the blunders of British military commanders and the government. The soldiers were sent food that had rotted away... a whole shipload of boots was delivered to the frontlines – all were for the left foot only. 9/10 of the British troops who perished in the Crimean War were killed not by Russian bullets, but by disease, neglect, and medical errors in British field hospitals.

The Fall of Sevastopol

Realizing that British soldiers were fighting and dying not for Britain, but for the political goal of "weakening Russia," the British public turned against the war. In January 1855, a little over a month after Tennyson's *Light Brigade* poem was published, a ***Snowball Riot*** occurred on Trafalgar Square in London. 1,500 people threw snowballs at the police demanding to stop the war. The Prime Minister resigned and peace negotiations began.

In 1857, as Queen Victoria was presenting the ***Victoria Cross*** to survivors of the Crimean War, alarming news was brought to her. A revolt against British colonial rule had broken out in India. This event became known as the ***Indian Mutiny***. India was ruled by the East India Company, which had its own military force. Part of this force was native Indian troops called ***Sepoys***. The East India Company bought them new rifles, and a rumor started circulating that these rifles required greased cartridges, and that the grease used in them was pig fat. Many among the Sepoys were Muslims and viewed pigs as unclean animals. They refused the new weapons, started a revolt, and captured Delhi, killing the British officers who commanded the Delhi Sepoy garrison and their families. British troops arrived and besieged Delhi for months, until they finally took it back.

Meanwhile the Indian Mutiny spread across the whole of Northern India. In ***Kanpur*** a few hundred British soldiers, their wives, kids, and servants found themselves under siege by rebels for 3 weeks. Over 250 died of hunger and wounds. The rest surrendered and were allowed to leave, but on their way to a boat on the Ganges River, the rebels massacred all the men and took women and kids back to the city where they were forced to work, gradually dying of hunger. A British force of 15 thousand troops was sent to save them, but before they reached Kanpur the rebels executed all the survivors and threw their bodies into a well.

When this news reached London, Queen Victoria's government stripped the East India Company of its status as a ruler of India and appointed a British *Viceroy* to govern India on behalf of the Queen. This form of direct British rule of India became known as **The British Raj** (from the Hindi word *rāj* = 'kingdom'), or the **Crown Rule**. In 1877, Queen Victoria was proclaimed the Empress of India. India was now viewed as the most valuable of British colonies – "the Jewel in the Crown." Queen Victoria started signing her name as "Victoria, R. I." – "Regina et Imperatrix" = "Queen & Empress" in Latin.

20 years after Victoria's coronation, her kids were becoming grownups. Her oldest son, Bertie (Albert) was in college, when Victoria learned that he was dating an actress. The royal parents were furious. Dating any 'commoner' was unthinkable for a future king. Plus, this reminded Victoria of her uncle, King William, who had 10 kids with his actress girlfriend, and, as a result, there was no heir for the throne. Victoria ordered her son to get rid of his actress girlfriend or else. This destroyed her relationship with Albert.

> ### *Viceroy*
> *A viceroy is the governor of a country or province ruling on behalf of a sovereign - a king or a queen. The word originated in the 16th century, made from the French words vice- 'in place of' + roi 'king'.*

The queen and Prince Albert enjoyed traveling around England and Scotland *incognito* (hiding their identity). Accompanied by a couple of their kids and friends, they pretended to be a regular middle class family, Mr. and Mrs. Churchill, and went from village to village with only two servants – no guards – staying at local inns. A few times they were found out by villagers who heard the royal servants call Victoria "Your Majesty." Once, a local band with drums and bagpipes suddenly marched to the inn where the royals were staying, and the Queen had to come out and receive flowers brought to her by the village kids. Throughout her reign Victoria was popular with the common people in Britain. She was cheerful, often laughed, and loved Charles Dickens' novels. She often went to the circus and made watercolor drawings of her kids and grandkids. Victoria's own government, however, preferred to keep her at a distance. Once, realizing that her Foreign Secretary was making war-and-peace decisions without informing her, Victoria dictated a letter to him, saying, "The Queen expects to be kept informed of what passes between the Foreign Secretary and the Foreign Ministers, before important decisions are taken." This demand seemed so out of place to the queen's lady-in-waiting who wrote down what the queen dictated, that she put the letter into her drawer and kept it there for 5 months before she dared to hand it to the Foreign Secretary.

In 1861 Queen Victoria's husband, Prince Albert, died of 'typhoid fever' – a disease caused by bacteria in food or water. With all city traffic relying on horses, the horse manure in the streets resulted in vast numbers of flies. Flies, dirty water, and unwashed hands spread typhoid. Albert's death was a blow from which Victoria never fully recovered. She stopped appearing in public, wore black for the rest of her life, and was nicknamed the 'Widow of Windsor.' After years of being absent from public life the queen was losing her popularity. In the streets of London there was talk of a republic, but the revolutionary mood was long gone. The rebels and the adventurers were busy building fortunes in the colonies.

Britain was now the leading industrial and trading nation of the world. In 1866 the ***Transatlantic telegraph cable*** connected England and America with instant communication. In 1869 the ***Suez Canal*** linked the Atlantic and Indian oceans. In the 1870s phones and postcards were already in everyday use and education was made compulsory (obligatory) for kids between 5 and 13 years of age in England and Wales. In 1867 the first bicycles and tricycles appeared in the streets of London! Queen Victoria herself rode a tricycle and started a bicycle-riding craze among women in Europe and America. Plus, the wealth of the far-flung colonies was pouring into British banks and, under their pressure, more and more resource-rich or strategically-attractive territories fell under British control. In 1861 the African king of Lagos, Nigeria, was summoned onboard of the British battleship HMS Prometheus docked at the Lagos port and informed that if he didn't sign the Treaty of Cession (ceding Lagos to the British crown), the Prometheus' cannons would reduce Lagos to a heap of rubble. The king signed the treaty. In the Pacific, the Fiji Islands were annexed in 1874. In the Mediterranean, Britain took control of Cyprus, following an 1878 secret agreement with Ottoman Turkey.

Did Queen Victoria approve of the ruthless British colonial policies? Certainly. While thousands of British troops, colonists, and native people in the colonies perished in brutal wars, the British public rarely glimpsed the real cost of the colonial expansion. They learned about the colonies at government-organized 'propaganda' events, like the ***Colonial and Indian Exhibition*** of 1886 in London that showed the goods imported from the colonies and the cultural treasures of the colonized lands. The political narrative of the British government convinced the public that British troops were 'liberating' the colonies from 'savage' native customs and bringing them 'freedom and civilization.'

The White Man's Burden

The ideology of the 'civilizing' mission of Europe was perfectly captured by the English poet Rudyard Kipling in his poem **The White Man's Burden**.

Take up the White Man's burden —
The savage wars of peace —
Fill full the mouth of Famine
And bid the sickness cease;
And when your goal is nearest
The end for others sought,
Watch Sloth and heathen Folly
Bring all your hopes to nought.

Jingoism

Along with the 'white man's burden,' another term related to the colonial political narrative became popular in Britain - 'jingoism.' Jingoism (adjective – 'jingoist') was used to describe the British public's enthusiasm for colonial wars – the cheering for sending British troops overseas to 'defend British interests.' The term came from an 1870s song about the rivalry between the Russian Empire (the 'Russian Bear') and Britain.

We don't want to fight,
but by Jingo if we do,
We've got the ships,
we've got the men,
we've got the money too!
We've fought the Bear before,
and while we're Britons true
The Russians shall not have
Constantinople!

'Jingo' stood for 'Jesus.' Since Christian teaching disapproves 'swearing' or making an 'oath,' especially calling on God's authority, people started deliberately mispronouncing words such as 'Jesus' or 'God.' The term for such word distortions is a **minced oath**. Modern examples: 'gee' (Jesus) and 'gosh' (God).

The opening of the Colonial and Indian Exhibition in London, 1886

"Victoria D.G. Britt. Reg. F.D."= Latin: "Victoria Dei Gratia Brittaniae Regina Fidei Defensor"= "Victoria by the Grace of God Queen of Britain, Protector of the Faith"
silver crown
1887–1892

British troops fighting the Zulus

In 1867, in South Africa, a little Dutch kid played with children of a local African tribe, and one of the native kids gave him a shiny rock found in the Orange River. The rock turned out to be a diamond of enormous value. Two years later a Dutch farmer paid a native tribe 500 sheep, 10 oxen, and a horse for another diamond found on the banks of the Orange River. It became known as the Star of South Africa. Its original uncut weight was 83.5 karats. It was cut to a gem of 47.69 carats (9.538 g). These finds resulted in a diamond rush, with hundreds of adventurers from all across Europe going to South Africa to mine for diamonds. In 1876 the diamond-rich areas were purchased and annexed by Britain under the pretext of defending the Dutch farmers – the Boers – from the Zulus, the native African tribes that were migrating south along the Eastern coast of Africa.

In the 17th century Portuguese colonists brought the culture of corn cultivation from America to Africa. Corn yielded bigger crops, but also required more water than native African grains. As a result, the Zulu population was rapidly growing and migrating South in search of well-watered lands. Zulu tribal society was organized around its military, with all young men and women conscripted into the army. As the Zulus migrated south, they destroyed other native tribes on their way. This expansion known as *Mfecane* (the "Crushing") depopulated large territories along the coast and led Zulus into conflict with British and Dutch settlers.

In 1879 Zulu King Cetshwayo led his forces against the British troops, beginning the *Anglo-Zulu War*. In the first battle of this war 15,000 Zulus attacked a British fort at Isandlwana and destroyed a 1,300-men British garrison. Once all the rifle ammunition was used up, the British commander ordered, "Fix bayonets and die like British soldiers." They all perished, but more British troops arrived and eventually the Zulus were defeated, King Cetshwayo was taken prisoner, and Zululand became part of the British colony of Natal.

King Cetshwayo

In 1882 captive King Cetshwayo was brought to London. Colonial authorities wanted Queen Victoria to appoint him a '**puppet**' ruler, who would make Zulus obey the British. To meet Victoria, Cetshwayo wore a coat, a top hat, but refused to wear shoes and went barefoot. Queen Victoria was a fine diplomat. She told him through an interpreter that she knew he was a great warrior. "I am rejoicing that we are now friends," she said. Later, asked by a reporter about the Queen, Cetshwayo graciously said, "She is born to rule men. She is like me. We are both rulers. She was very kind to me and I will always think of her."

In 1880 the Boers of the Transvaal hoisted the Dutch flag and declared Transvaal independent from the British. The British governor of Natal rushed to put down the Boer uprising, but was killed by the Boers along with his 400 men. The British government backed off and Transvaal was given back to the Boers.

But in the colonial world peace was short-lived. Two more brutal wars broke out – in Egypt and in Afghanistan. In 1879 Lord Lytton, the British governor-general of India, suspected that the Afghan emir, a son of Dost Mohammad, was getting too friendly with the Russians, and decided to teach him a lesson by invading Afghanistan from India. British troops occupied the Afghan capital, Kabul, and the emir fled. But soon Afghans rebelled, and a second British invasion force had to be sent from India.

Meanwhile in Egypt, the army overthrew the country's Turkish ruler – the **Khedive** of Egypt and Sudan – for paying native Arab officers far less than the European **mercenaries** (soldiers-for-hire). The British government sent troops to Egypt – supposedly, to protect the Suez Canal, but, of course, there was another reason... The British Liberal Party needed a boost in popularity to compete with the conservatives. So the liberal politicians decided that a 'war protecting British interests' would make them look patriotic and bring the voters to their side.

However, after the army rebellion, native Muslim Egyptians rioted in Alexandria claiming that the government sacrificed their interests in favor of Europeans and Christians. 50 Europeans and 125 native Egyptian Christians were killed. This tragedy was exactly what the Liberal Party wanted. Now they had a moral justification for war. British warships started a 10-hour non-stop bombardment of the military forts of Alexandria, turning most of the city into ruins. Soon more British troops arrived, marched inland and took over Egypt. Queen Victoria's son, the Duke of Connaught, participated in the war, leading a British brigade.

Another chapter of the Anglo-Egyptian wars was the uprising in Sudan, led by Muslim religious leader Muhammad Ahmad, who proclaimed himself *mahdi* – the 'Final Leader' – who would bring Muslims to rule the world. British commander General Gordon, with a small number of troops, tried to evacuate Europeans and Egyptian garrisons from Sudan, but ended up besieged in Khartoum by the rebels for almost a year. The Khartoum garrison was growing smaller and smaller – soldiers were dying of wounds and tropical diseases. Every night Gordon spent on the palace roof, "alone with his duty and his God," hoping to see the British rescue mission coming. The mission arrived 2 days after Khartoum fell and Gordon was killed. Gordon's last entry in his diary was, "I have done my best for the honor of our country. Good-bye." Queen Victoria wrote to Gordon's sister, "Dear Miss Gordon, how shall I write to you, or how shall I attempt to express what I feel! To think of your dear, noble, heroic brother, who served his country and his Queen so truly, so heroically, with such a self-sacrifice, not having been rescued! That the promises of support were not fulfilled, which I so frequently and constantly demanded of those who sent him on his mission, is to me grief inexpressible."

"Gordon's Last Stand" and a photograph of Queen Victoria from 1897

Gordon, like so many other British officers who perished in faraway colonies, became a symbol of British heroism – serving his country, "faithful unto death." Few Brits of the Victorian era wondered, what were those 'British interests' for which heroes like Gordon died? Certainly, these were not the interests of common citizens, but of the banks and British companies importing raw materials and natural resources from the colonies and selling British goods to the colonists and the native elites.

In 1887 London and the whole kingdom celebrated Queen Victoria's **Jubilee** – 50 years on the throne. 10 years later they celebrated her 'Diamond Jubilee' – 60 years on the throne. Victoria died in 1901 at the age of 81. Her last wish was to be buried wearing a white wedding dress and her wedding veil.

"We are not amused"

"We are not amused" is a famous phrase attributed to Queen Victoria. Supposedly, she used these words to express her disapproval upon hearing some gossip she found inappropriate. This story comes from a memoir by one of Victoria's court ladies, and it's not clear whether it actually happened. According to Victoria's granddaughter, Alice, the Queen herself denied ever having said "We are not amused."

Left: Queen Victoria's Osborne House interior; Below: Ruins of Alexandria after the British bombardment; Victorian tricycle

Napoleon III
1808 – 1873

Napoleon III by Franz Xaver Winterhalter

Charles-Louis Napoleon Bonaparte – Napoleon III – was the son of Napoleon Bonaparte's brother Louis and the daughter of Napoleon's wife Josephine (from her 1st marriage). After the defeat of Napoleon I, his family had to leave France. So Louis Napoleon grew up in Switzerland, went to school in Germany, and, when he was 15, moved to Italy. In Italy he got involved with the *Carbonari*, secret societies of Italian revolutionaries who were preparing an uprising against the Austrian occupation of Northern Italy. When the Austrians started hunting and arresting Carbonari, Louis Napoleon and his mom escaped to France which was in the middle of the 1830 July Revolution. King Charles X, a brother of Louis XVI, was overthrown, and a member of the French royal Bourbon family, Louis Philippe, was proclaimed king. Louis Philippe didn't allow young Louis Napoleon to remain in Paris, but during the few days of his stay there, to his great surprise, a crowd of people assembled in front of his hotel, proclaiming their support for Napoleon Bonaparte's dynasty. That's when Louis Napoleon realized that the fame and legacy of his uncle could win him the throne.

Back in Switzerland, Louis Napoleon joined the Swiss army and became an officer. He also started writing down his own political philosophy, in which he tried to reconcile the two opposing political movements in France – the supporters of the republic and the supporters of the monarchy. He called his set of ideas "the principle of popular sovereignty." A powerful and caring monarch can protect the interests of the people better than a government of a republic, he concluded. His *constitutional empire* was supposed to be "strong without despotism, free without anarchy, independent without conquest." Louis Napoleon wrote books and articles promoting these ideas. They became popular and were translated into all major European languages. In 1836 Louis Napoleon tried to organize a military coup d'etat against Louis Philippe, but failed and escaped back to Switzerland. Meanwhile, his popularity in France was growing – with the help of... Louis Philippe himself.

Supporters of monarchy – monarchists – despised Louis Philippe, because he didn't inherit the throne, but was put on the throne by a revolution, and even nicknamed 'Citizen King.' His support came from the wealthy industrialists and bankers – very uncool for a king. Parisians got into the habit of making rude remarks about the king – loudly – while passing directly under the Tuileries Palace windows. To escape insults, Louis Philippe had to dig a moat, plant a thick hedge, and install an iron railing between the palace walls and the street. To improve his image Louis Philippe tried to present himself as a figure similar to Napoleon, whose career was also launched by a revolution. He brought Napoleon's body from Saint Helena to France, returned Napoleon's statue to the **Vendome Column**, and in 1836 opened the **Arc de Triomphe** (Triumphal Arch) dedicated to French victories in the Napoleonic wars.

In 1840 Louis Napoleon attempted another coup. Having no plan except the expectation that the French army would side with him to honor the memory of Napoleon I, Louis Napoleon sailed from England with only 50 men, and a pet eagle, which was supposed to perch on his banner as the symbol of victory. The adventure ended in a complete failure and Louis Napoleon was locked up in jail, where he wrote poetry and political articles for newspapers and magazines. Six years later his doctor smuggled a workman's clothes into his cell, and, disguised as a firewood delivery man, Louis Napoleon walked out of prison and left for England. In 1848 another revolution erupted in Paris. Armed rioters demanding restoration of the republic clashed with French troops. A few rebels were killed and the crowds carried their bodies all around the city, shouting "Vengeance!" Barricades were being built on every street from paving stones and furniture. The crowds rushed to the Tuileries, and Louis Philippe abdicated the throne. Just as he crossed the English channel escaping to England, Louis Napoleon headed in the opposite direction – to Paris.

Napoleon III daguerrotype (early type of photograph), 1851

"Lamartine rejects the red flag in front of the Town Hall of Paris" by Henri Félix Emmanuel Philippoteaux

In Paris, a ***provisional government*** was assembled. One of its members, French poet and political thinker Alphonse de Lamartine, confronted the rioters from the Tuileries palace balcony. "What do you want?" he asked. "Your head!" screamed the rioters. But Lamartine wasn't scared. "I wish you had this thing on YOUR shoulders," he responded, pointing at his head. The rioters admired his courage, laughed, and demanded to replace the French tricolor with the "red flag of the revolution." But Lamartine had something to say about that idea as well. "The tricolor flag has gone around the world during the Republic and Empire for your liberties and glory, while your red flag has only gone around Paris, drenched in the blood of the innocent people massacred by the revolution of 1789!" The rioters calmed down and agreed to support new elections with voting rights for every French citizen over 21, and a new constitution. The constitution of 1848 made an elected president the head of the French Republic, limiting his authority to one term of 4 years. During the elections, French military commander General Cavaignac received 1,400,000 votes, but Louis Napoleon got 5,400,000 votes and became the first president of the Second Republic.

In 1851 Louis Napoleon's presidential term ended, and the constitution did not allow a second term. So, the "Prince-President" ordered the secret arrest of his main competitors and dissolved the French Assembly. Again, there were barricades and blood in the streets, but Napoleon had the support of the army, and his coup d'etat succeeded. Soon, under the slogan "the Empire is peace" Louis Napoleon proclaimed himself "Napoleon III, Emperor of the French." His next task was to get married and have a kid – the heir to the new empire. While studying the list of European princesses available for marriage, the 45-year-old Louis Napoleon also flirted with ladies at his own court. He paid a lot of attention to one of them, 27-year-old Spanish noblewoman Eugénie Montijo. Eugénie asked a family friend for advice on how to handle the situation. The friend happened to be the famous French writer – the star of French Romanticism – Prosper Mérimée. He rehearsed with Eugénie every possible scenario of conversations with the emperor. So, when Louis Napoleon asked her, "What is the road to your heart?" Eugénie replied, "Through the chapel, my lord," – that is, only through marriage. A few days later Napoleon proposed. Two weeks later the couple was married and Eugénie became empress. Napoleon and Eugénie had a son, Louis, "the Prince Imperial."

Despite his "The Empire is peace" slogan, Napoleon III didn't hesitate to send French troops to war. He owed his crown to the army, and the French war machine needed wars to grow its power and wealth. Plus, Napoleon himself dreamed of living up to the military glory of Napoleon I and his idol, Julius Caesar, whose portrait by the French Neoclassical painter Jean-Auguste Ingres decorated his office. Napoleon III started his quest for military glory by provoking Russia to clash with the Ottoman Empire, and then dragged it into the infamous Crimean War. Thousands of French troops died on the battlefields of Crimea, winning nothing for their country except a vague political advantage over the Russian Empire.

Next came the war in Italy. Some kingdoms in Italy were independent, but Central Italy was ruled by the Pope, and Northern Italy was still occupied by Austria. Italians asked France to help them gain full independence, and Napoleon didn't mind helping, but there was one big problem. Italians wanted to get rid not only of the Austrians, but also of the Pope's rule in Central Italy.

Empress Eugenie

The French Catholic Church, Napoleon's government, and Empress Eugénie were all against the invasion of Italy. Italians, however, had a plan. The Prime Minister of the Italian Kingdom of Piedmont-Sardinia came to Paris bringing with him his beautiful cousin Virginia Oldoini. Predictably, Napoleon III fell in love with her and his marriage was destroyed. For a couple years Virginia reported all Napoleon's moods and ideas to Italians and tried to talk him into invading Italy. Way to be a spy!

In 1858, when Napoleon III and Eugénie were going to the opera, three explosive devices were thrown at their carriage killing 8 royal guards and passers-by. To prevent panic, Napoleon and Eugénie showed up at the theater like nothing happened, but the crowd at the opera already knew and applauded them. The conspirators turned out to be Italian nationalists upset with Napoleon III for failing to help Italians in their fight for independence. The would-be assassin was tried and executed, but Napoleon III finally made up his mind, and soon French troops joined the Sardinian army in Northern Italy. A number of battles were won. Napoleon III and his generals weren't the equals of Napoleon I, but Austrian commanders were even worse. As if to illustrate the saying "Victory comes to the army that makes the fewest blunders," the French won. As a result, a bunch of Northern Italian lands were added to the Kingdom of Sardinia, while France got the provinces of Nice and Savoy. Yes, Nice and Savoy used to be in Italy! Napoleon III also placed 20,000 French troops in Rome to protect the Pope from Italians.

Virginia Oldoini

Like his uncle Napoleon I, Napoleon III relied on the arts and design to glorify his rule and make his court and government look truly 'imperial.'

The Palais Garnier Opera opened in 1975.

Uniforms of officials were covered in gold embroidery, and palace guards looked like actors wearing costumes, rather than military men. Court balls gathered over 5 thousand guests, and by the end of the evening Empress Eugénie could hardly walk, exhausted from wearing enormous amounts of jewelry, a heavy gold-embroidered gown, and a massive gold crown. The Empress's 'Mondays' – gatherings of intellectuals and friends of the royal family – became famous all over Europe. During the hunting parties held by the court in the fall, female guests were required to wear at least 15 new gowns. To avoid wasting money on these, many women pretended to be sick rather than accept the invitation.

Empress Eugénie was a huge fan of Marie Antoinette. She collected Marie Antoinette's jewelry and personal items and made the Louis XVI -style furniture and decor popular in Europe. But most of all Eugénie was interested in fashion. When spectacular dresses created for her by famous designers were delivered to her, she didn't hesitate to cut and alter them to fit her own sense of style. Nicknamed the 'Queen of Fashion,' Eugénie never wore the same dress twice. So many outfits were made for her, that she regularly held charity sales of her clothes to make room for new stuff. In the 1860s Eugénie stopped wearing dresses with huge crinolines (hoops supporting the skirt) and switched to a narrow dress silhouette with a 'bustle' – fabric gathered on the back of the skirt. All of Europe followed the evolution of Eugénie's fashion look. Women imitated her hairstyles, use of colors and accessories. Eugénie-inspired fashion was known as *à l'impératrice* – 'like the empress.'

Napoleon III's dining room at the Louvre Palace

Empress Eugenie attends the investiture of Napoleon III with the Order of the Garter;
Left: a bustle; Below: a painting by French Impressionist artist Pierre-Auguste Renoir

Napoleon III started the reconstruction of Paris, replacing narrow medieval lanes with wide streets and grand boulevards. Rivers were dressed in stone embankments and dams were built to prevent floods. Napoleon III also wanted to be seen as a patron of the arts and an intellectual. In 1863, the **Paris Salon**, the annual art exhibition of the French Academy of Arts, rejected the works of **avant-garde** French artists, including Édouard Manet and Camille Pissarro. The artists complained, and Napoleon III ordered that they should be allowed to hold their own art show. This began the trend of **Impressionism** in art. Napoleon III also promoted ideas that were supposed to improve the life of the working people. French workers received the right to go on strike. The employers were prohibited from writing negative comments in the employees' work permits – the practice that prevented employees from quitting their job for fear they wouldn't find a new one once their work document has a negative 'recommendation.' In 1861 the first French woman received a university degree. A prize was promised for creating a cheap substitute for butter, and it was won in 1869 by a product named 'oleomargarine' – modern margarine.

Avant-garde = *new and experimental. The term comes from French. Its original meaning is the "vanguard" – the troops at the head of an army.*

Under Napoleon III France waged a number of colonial wars. Some invasions were done under the pretext of defending Christianity. France sent troops to Syria to – supposedly – protect Syrian Christians from the Turks, and to China – to "make the Chinese respect Christian missionaries." Actually, the war with China – fought along with Britain – was the *Second Opium War* (1856-1860) whose goal was to force the Chinese Qing dynasty to allow selling opium drugs prohibited by Chinese law. Joint British and French forces landed in China, took Beijing, and ordered the troops to loot and burn the historic Imperial Summer Palace, *Yuanmingyuan*. 300 servants and court ladies perished in the flames. Precious art and centuries-worth of cultural treasures stored in the palace were gone within hours. In 1862 France conquered Cochinchina – Southern Vietnam, including Saigon. In 1863 the French took over Cambodia.

Next, in 1863, Napoleon III saw an opportunity in Mexico. The United States was weakened by the American Civil War, so England, Spain, and France sent their fleets to attack the Mexican coast. Soon England and Spain negotiated a deal with Mexico, but Napoleon III wanted to install a 'puppet' ruler, Austrian prince Maximilian, as the Emperor of Mexico – to make Mexico a French protectorate. However, Mexican Republicans led by President Benito Juáres refused to play along, and the United States pointed Napoleon III to the door, reminding him of America's famous *Monroe Doctrine* that did not permit any European intrusion in American affairs. Napoleon withdrew the French troops, abandoning his 'puppet.' Maximilian was executed by the Mexicans.

A Puppet Ruler claims to be elected / appointed by his people and to serve its country. In reality, the 'puppet' was installed by another, more powerful country, and follows orders from abroad.

Ruins of Yuanmingyuan, the Old Summer Palace

> **The Monroe Doctrine**
>
> The Monroe Doctrine was developed by President James Monroe in 1823. It's a US foreign policy principle stating that any political or military intrusion by European powers anywhere in the Americas shall be viewed as an attack on the United States.
>
> **A Protectorate** is a state controlled by another state that also provides its military protection.

The disaster in Mexico undermined Napoleon's reputation as a statesman. He was becoming less and less popular. Trying to prevent yet another revolution, he went for some democratic reforms, but that didn't help much. He was ridiculed and despised. Napoleon III had a lot of personal courage, but it was based on his firm belief in *predestination*. Just like his uncle, Napoleon I, he felt that he owed his success to fate and luck that somehow belonged to the Bonaparte family. He secretly visited well-known fortune tellers in Paris, and believed their predictions. Empress Eugénie avoided facing reality as well. She was taking huge quantities of chloral hydrate – a *sedative* drug (to sedate = to calm down) discovered in the early XIX century and used in mental hospitals. Popular among wealthy French women as a treatment for insomnia, chloral hydrate was highly addictive. It also caused depression, anxiety and mood swings.

Finally, Napoleon's advisors suggested that, in order to preserve his empire, he should look for another war – not in some faraway colony, but close to home. The war would shift public attention from problems at home to fighting an external enemy, raising a wave of patriotism that the emperor could ride.

There was a good candidate for an enemy – Prussia. Prussia defeated Austria in 1866 and became the center of German unification. Its power was growing, as more and more German states were joining its coalition. Prussians were also trying to put their own 'puppet,' a German prince, on the Spanish throne – to create a German-Spanish alliance against France. Empress Eugénie, a Spaniard herself, was outraged and called for war, convinced that a new French weapon, the *mitrailleuse* (an early *machine gun* that shot 25 rounds in rapid succession) would sweep away German armies. Looking for sensational news, the French *yellow press* (cheap gossip-focused newspapers) presented war on Prussia as a done deal. So in 1870 Napoleon III declared war on Prussia. It was a blunder that cost him his throne. The deputies of the Corps Legislatif, the lower house of the French parliament, voted for war 246 to 10.

The 250 members of the French Senate all voted for war, summing up their position with an address to the emperor: "Your Majesty draws the sword, and the whole country goes with you." In an address to the nation, Napoleon III said, "There are in the life of peoples solemn moments, when the national honor, violently excited, presses itself irresistibly, rises above all other interests, and applies itself to the single purpose of directing the destinies of the nation. One of these decisive hours has now arrived for France." Accompanied by his 14-year-old son, Napoleon left for the war in the middle of patriotic celebrations. In the streets of Paris crowds chanted "On to Berlin!" Napoleon III even appointed a day for a victory parade in Berlin – August 15th, his birthday. And so started the war that cost France about 130,000 French soldiers killed, 143,000 wounded, plus thousands of civilian casualties.

The Prussian chancellor Otto von Bismarck was thrilled. He couldn't wait for the war. German armies were well-trained, well-armed and highly motivated. The French started losing. A British newspaper correspondent reported from the frontlines: "The emperor behaves as if he doesn't care if he dies. He actually throws himself in death's way...A shell exploded a few feet in front of him, but he continued on his way without showing the slightest emotion." Realizing that he was useless on the battlefields, Napoleon decided to go home to Paris, but received the following telegram from his wife: "Don't even think of coming back unless you want to unleash a terrible revolution. They will say you quit the army to flee the danger."

After a number of defeats, Napoleon III decided to personally lead his army into battle. He had zero experience as a military commander and was barely on his feet, sick with the flu. He lost the **Battle of Sedan**, ordered to raise the white flag, and surrendered along with 104,000 of his soldiers.

Vintage prints depicting Napoleon III surrendering his sword to Bismarck and King Wilhelm of Prussia

"My lord and brother," he wrote that day to King Wilhelm of Prussia, "not having been able to die in the midst of my troops, the only thing I can do is to place my sword in the hands of your Majesty. Your Majesty's good brother, Napoleon." King Wilhelm responded, "My lord and brother, regretting the circumstances under which we meet, I accept the sword of your Majesty, and I pray you to name one of your officers provided with full powers to negotiate for the capitulation of the army which has so bravely fought under your command. Your Majesty's good brother, Wilhelm." Empress Eugénie was far less generous than King Wilhelm. When she heard the news, her reaction was: "No! An emperor does not capitulate!... Why didn't he kill himself? Doesn't he know he has dishonored himself?!" Outside the Tuileries Palace an American journalist wrote this report, "Paris is in a state of riotous excitement. Crowds are tearing down the imperial arms, and destroying the golden eagles of the empire. We fear the city will soon be at the mercy of mobs."

Not all of the French army surrendered with Napoleon. Part of it was under siege in the town of Metz. Germans paraded 104,000 French prisoners who surrendered with Napoleon in front of the Metz fortress. The morale (fighting spirit) of the French troops hit the floor, and the war was lost for the French. The French public blamed Napoleon III for the defeat, and revolutionary riots broke out all over France. In Paris crowds stormed the Tuileries Palace, and Empress Eugénie barely escaped, having hidden in the palace art gallery. Minutes later the crowds broke the doors of the palace, looted the royal apartments and wrote insulting graffiti on the walls and on the sculptures. Eugénie wandered around Paris with only 3 francs in her pocket, knocking on the doors of her friends – none of whom appeared to be home... The only person who dared to help her was an American, the royal family's dentist, who took Eugénie to the coast where she boarded a yacht departing for England. Remnants of French armies continued resistance led by the new French government – the Government of National Defense that declared the end of the empire and established the **Third Republic**. Napoleon III met with King Wilhelm of Prussia who gave him the Castle of Wilhelmshohe as his residence while the emperor was a prisoner of war. Napoleon's son, the Prince Imperial, escaped – thanks to his teacher, who, at the last moment, put him on a train departing for Belgium. From Belgium the prince sailed to England, where he joined his mom, Eugénie.

Prussian troops, Franco-Prussian War

Looking back, Napoleon III blamed the French public for starting the war. In an interview for the *The London Telegraph* while in captivity, he said: "L'homme propose, mais Dieu dispose (French for "Man proposes, but God decides"). I had no wish to make war. It was chance that brought it. Public opinion was ignited in its favor, and I had to agree to the wish of the people." Napoleon III was released and joined his family 6 months later. The Prussian army surrounded Paris and started a four and a half-month siege.

Napoleon III died in 1873. His son perished in 1879 while fighting in the British colonial war against the Zulu tribes in South Africa.

'Man proposes, but God decides'

'Man proposes, but God decides' is a translation of the Latin "Homo proponit, sed Deus disponit" from The Imitation of Christ – a 15th-century Christian devotional book by the German priest Thomas à Kempis.

Empress Eugenie's crown; Eugenie and Russian Emperor Alexander II at a party at Tuileries Palace; photograph of Eugenie, 1856

OTTO VON BISMARCK
1815 – 1898

Otto Von Bismarck was a German statesman who played a key role in the unification of Germany. He was born to a family of Prussian *junkers* (pronounced 'ioonkers' = land owners) in Pomerania. The family was far from wealthy. As a young man Otto studied law, but was rarely seen at the university lectures. He preferred hunting, military arts, flirting with girls, and drinking with fellow students. Combined, these interests had potentially lethal consequences in the 19th century! Sure enough, during his first year at the university Otto fought 28 duels and barely survived!

Having graduated, Bismarck briefly worked for the local government and then left to manage his family's estate in Pomerania, learn farming, and do more hunting and flirting.

Junker

The junkers were members of the land-owning nobility in Prussia. The word comes from the German 'jung' (young) and 'Herr' (lord).

Duel

A duel is an arranged fight between two people. In the 17th century, inspired by the ideals of chivalry, duels became a standard way for European noblemen to defend their 'honor' and settle disputes. If a man was challenged to a duel and rejected the challenge, he was ridiculed as someone who 'lost his honor.' By the end of the 18th century duellists switched from swords to pistols. They also started choosing 'seconds' – friends who attempted to reconcile them, and if reconciliation failed, arranged the terms for a duel. The culture of dueling disappeared by the mid 19th century.

When people met Bismarck, they were under the impression that he was a typical provincial German land owner interested only in country life, dogs, hunting, and drinking with his buddies. In reality, Bismarck was an avid reader, deeply interested in world politics and diplomacy. He was a good conversationalist, and enjoyed learning foreign languages. By the time he became known as a politician, he spoke English, French, Italian, Polish, and Russian. Bismarck got married, and the marriage was happy. He and his wife, Johanna, had 3 kids.

Prussia was a constitutional monarchy. When Bismarck was 32 he was elected to the Prussian parliament, the Landtag (also called the Diet). In 1848, as a wave of revolutions shook Europe, Prussian King Frederick Wilhelm IV agreed to a constitution and partial freedom of the press.

Liberal and socialist views were growing in popularity among intellectuals and politicians across Europe, but Bismarck stood out as a hard-core conservative who didn't care about liberal public opinion. He was a royalist and believed in the ***Divine Right*** of kings (the idea that kings are given authority by God). In the Landtag Bismarck fought against the liberal revolutionary forces and even tried to get the farmers who lived on his estate to form a militia and march on Berlin. "Away with the cities. I hope to see them all leveled to the ground," he declared.

Bismarck's royalism was not based on theory. It was rooted in the fact that Prussia owed a lot to its royal family, the Hohenzollerns. While French, British, and Russian royalty lived in ornate gilded palaces and wasted whole fortunes on balls, evening gowns, and art collections, the Hohenzollerns spent all the money arriving in the treasury on training a powerful army built on brutal discipline. The royal family's own lifestyle wasn't different from that of any common German landowner – like Bismarck. As a result, from a poor, isolated country with no natural resources Prussia rose as one of the most powerful European states. In the mid 19th century Germany still consisted of many kingdoms and princedoms, loosely organized into the German Confederation, and although the idea of unification was in the air, the two biggest German states – Prussia and Austria – opposed it. Bismarck's own thinking evolved from rejecting unification to promoting it as the only way to get ahead of the other European empires – Britain, France, and Russia. And he saw only one method for achieving German unification – war.

In the late 1850s Bismarck served as the Prussian ambassador in Russia and also in France. He was praised for his superb diplomatic skills, but he took no credit for his successes. "The longer I work in politics," he wrote, "the less I value human judgment. I look at things according to my human understanding, but I am grateful for God's help which gives me confidence that the Lord is able to turn our errors to our own good. Every day I experience this and feel humbled down."

Bismarck kept learning foreign languages and studied the cultures and customs of peoples across Europe in great depth. American poet and traveler Bayard Taylor recorded the following story. One day, at a restaurant, Bismarck noticed that a couple ladies sitting at a table next to him recognized him and immediately switched from German to the Latvian language. Latvia had been a Polish province, but after the ***Third Partition*** (division) ***of Poland*** in 1895, it became part of Russia. Many influential Latvian families had moved to Germany where they didn't feel at home. Bismarck quickly realized that the ladies had nothing positive to say about him, so he told his friend, "When I say something to you in a foreign language, hand me that plate of potatoes." Next he announced loudly in Latvian: "Pass the potatoes, please!" The friend handed him the potatoes. Embarrassed, the Latvian ladies quickly left the restaurant.

Bismarck is quoted as having said, "Great men have great dogs." He loved dogs and took his favorite Great Danes wherever he went. He believed that one of his dogs, Sultan, could tell if a person had good or bad intentions. When Sultan disliked someone, Bismarck was very suspicious. In St.Petersburg he was given a bear cub. The little bear named Mishka (a Russian affectionate word for a bear, a diminutive form of 'Michael') was present at all dinners and receptions in Bismarck's house and was allowed to climb on the dinner table and annoy servants.

In 1861 Prussian King Frederick Wilhelm IV died. His son Wilhelm inherited the throne and right away clashed with the Prussian parliament. The Landtag was dominated by liberal, pro-republic deputies. Wilhelm was advised that there was only one politician capable of resolving the crisis – Bismarck. So the king agreed to appoint Otto von Bismarck Minister President and Foreign Minister. Now Bismarck had the freedom and authority he needed to pursue his true goal – the creation of the German Empire. The liberals in the Prussian Diet kept getting in Bismarck's way, so he convinced the king to dissolve the Diet and used his authority to restrict the freedom of the press. Newspapers couldn't criticize the government the way they used to. In his famous 1862 *Iron and Blood* speech, Bismarck declared that "The great questions of our time will not be resolved by speeches and majority decisions – but by iron and blood."

One afternoon, in 1866, walking alone down Unter den Linden ('Under the limetrees') Boulevard in Berlin, Bismarck heard a couple gunshots, turned around and saw a young man with a revolver aiming at him. Bismarck rushed to the man and grabbed his right hand as he shot again. The assassin quickly passed the revolver from right to left hand and shot two more times but, with Bismarck holding him, he missed. Bismarck handed the assassin over to the police, went home and had dinner with his family like nothing happened. The assassin, a German liberal, committed suicide in prison. Many among the German liberal public openly expressed their disappointment that Bismarck survived, prompting conservatives to unite even more resolutely around Bismarck.

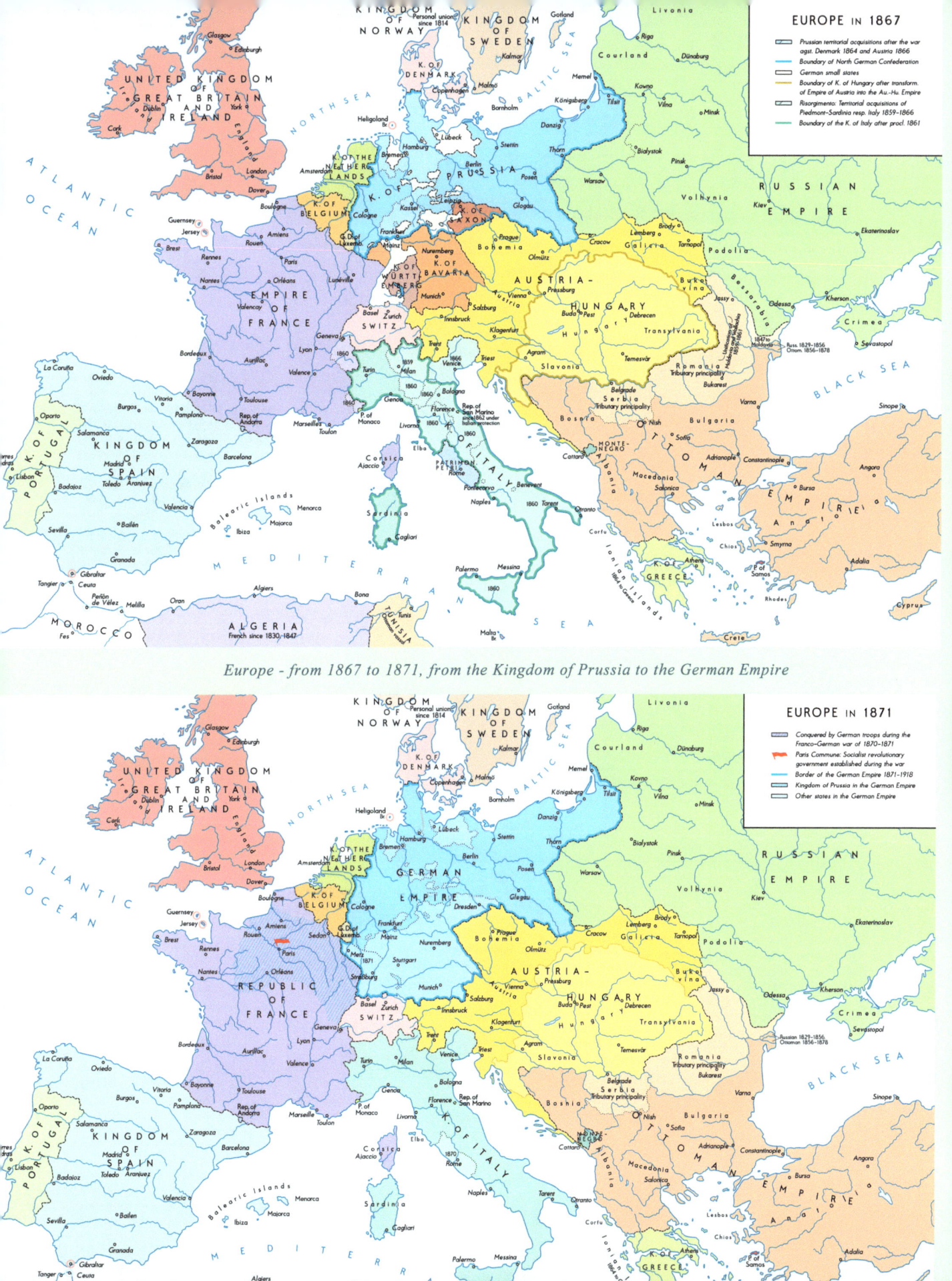

Bismarck meant it when he spoke about "iron and blood." To him, war was a tool and he was ready to use it. Bismarck's biographer George Hesekiel wrote, "The times were growing more serious. Minds began to feel that stillness that precedes the storm. 'Mit Gott für König und Vaterland!' (German, 'With God for the King and the Fatherland!') – this ancient royal battle cry first crept softly, and then louder and louder, from mouth to mouth, from heart to heart, until at last it thundered in the roaring of a thousand cannons throughout the trembling world."

First, there was a clash with Denmark over a couple disputed princedoms – Schleswig and Holstein. Prussia and Austria joined forces and defeated Denmark. Austrians expected that the two princedoms would become independent members of the German Confederation, but Bismarck – a brilliant diplomat – imposed his own solution: Prussia was to rule Schleswig, and Austria was to rule Holstein. Austrians protested, and Bismarck saw this as an opportunity to provoke them to war. He wanted Austria out of the way, so Germany could unify around Prussia. Bismarck reached out to Napoleon III to see what his reaction would be if Prussia went to war with Austria. Napoleon asked if he could have some German territories bordering on France in exchange for neutrality. Bismarck said 'no', but if Napoleon wanted to grab a chunk of Belgium, nobody would mind. Rumors of these negotiations reached Austria. In no time the Austrian ambassador was in front of Bismark: "What's going on?" "Nothing," replied Bismarck, "and you certainly don't expect me to tell you if I, indeed, intend to do what you think I am planning to do." This story brings to mind one of the most famous Bismarck quotes: "Never believe anything in politics until it has been officially denied."

In 1866 Austria was finally cornered into declaring war on Prussia. Bismarck promptly sent troops to annex Schleswig, triggering the *Seven Weeks' War*. Prussia won, and while patriotic Prussians and the king demanded the army march on Vienna, Bismarck instead insisted on a *soft peace* – no victory parade, no humiliation for Austrians. His goal was achieved – Germany was unified around Prussia. Bismarck's decision not to conquer Austria is a famous example of *Realpolitik* – a realistic, pragmatic way of taking political decisions. Austria had to form a new alliance: In 1867 it joined with the Kingdom of Hungary to be ruled by one monarch, forming the Austro-Hungarian Empire. During the Seven Weeks' War Bismarck was given the military rank of major-general, and from then on he always appeared in public wearing a military uniform, even though he never fought in a single battle.

The **Franco-Prussian War** was another brilliant political scheme. Bismarck was concerned that France would not allow Germany to complete its unification. It could join forces with Austria, or with the anti-Prussian party in Bavaria, or, even worse, with liberals and socialists in Prussia itself. So France had to go. When – suddenly – the Spanish throne became available, Bismarck demanded it for Leopold of Hohenzollern, a Prussian prince related to Spanish royalty. Napoleon III took the bait and declared war on Prussia. After only a few months the war was over, Napoleon III surrendered at the Battle of Sedan, and – just like that – the Prussian army was marching toward Paris. Despite its short duration, the Franco-Prussion War was absolutely brutal. An American physician, Dr.Sims, who was present at the battle of Sedan, wrote: "The newspaper reports of the cruelty of the Prussians are not in the least exaggerated. The particulars are not fit for publication. Some 80,000 French prisoners marched from Sedan to the little peninsula formed by the river...if I lived a hundred years, I could never forget what I saw them endure. They spent several days there on that piece of land, dying of sickness and starvation...The Bavarians utterly destroyed Bazeilles, a town of 3000 inhabitants. They say they were fired upon from the windows of the houses. In their rage they barred the doors, and set fire to each house, burning a great number of women and children. They also shot a priest there, and some nuns and school-girls..."

> ## *Realpolitik*
>
> *Realpolitik (German for 'realistic politics') is a practical approach to making political decisions. It suggests that political decisions should be based on the given circumstances, not on ideological or moral considerations. The two most famous examples of realpolitik decisions taken by Bismarck are the 'soft peace' with Austria and the social reforms Bismarck introduced to slow down the growth of socialism in Germany, even though, as a conservative, he was opposed to all reforms. "Politics is the art of the possible, the attainable, the art of the next best," he wrote.*

When the white flag of surrender was raised on the citadel of Sedan and the French army commander came out to negotiate with the Germans, Bismarck was there. The Germans demanded the unconditional surrender of the whole army. Only the French officers would be allowed to keep their swords. The French commander asked for more favorable terms. He couldn't allow his whole army to become prisoners of war. It would be wise of Prussia to show generosity, he told Bismarck. That would earn the gratitude of the French nation, and become the foundation of lasting peace. He was instantly sorry for his request, because Bismarck had quite a bit to say on the subject. "You [the French] are an irritable and jealous nation," he said, "envious and jealous to the utmost degree. You have not forgiven us Sadowa [the decisive battle of the Austro-Prussian War], so how are you going to forgive us Sedan?"

Then another French general came forward saying he had a message from Napoleon III. The emperor sent his sword to the King of Prussia as a sign of surrender, hoping that the king would appreciate the gesture and grant France a more honorable capitulation. "And whose, exactly, sword is that?" inquired Bismarck. "The sword of France or Napoleon's own? If it's the sword of France, then we can negotiate." "It's only the sword

Napoleon III and Bismarck the morning after surrender. Below: Prussian Iron Cross 2nd Class and 1870-71 Campaign Medal

of the Emperor," the general replied. Bismarck raised his eyebrows in disdain and agreed to move the surrender deadline from 4 AM to 9 AM the next morning, and that was it.

Next morning, before breakfast, Napoleon himself left the fortress of Sedan in a carriage, accompanied by only 6 officers. He asked Bismark to arrange his meeting with the King of Prussia. But Bismarck told him the king was away and not available (actually he was only 10 miles away from Sedan). They went to a farm cottage nearby, sat in front of it and smoked together. Bismarck asked if Napoleon could negotiate peace on behalf of France, but the emperor said he viewed himself as a prisoner, not a representative of his country. Bismarck should negotiate with the French government in Paris. Indeed, soon came the news that revolutionaries had taken control of Paris and proclaimed a republic.

In January 1871 in the grand Hall of Mirrors of the Versailles Palace, Prussian King Wilhelm I was proclaimed **Kaiser** (emperor) of the German **Reich** (kingdom/empire). Smaller German states gave up their independence and joined Prussia, which also annexed two French provinces – Alsace and Lorraine. The German Empire was a constitutional monarchy. Its parliament was now called the **Reichstag**. Bismarck was appointed the Imperial Chancellor (**Reichskanzler**).

Kaiser, Tsar, Caesar

German 'Kaiser' and Russian 'Tsar' both come from the name of Julius Caesar following the tradition of using 'Caesar' as the title of every Roman emperor.

The Prussian army besieged Paris, and once the French government signed the capitulation, German troops entered the city. A German victory parade in Paris was one of the conditions of capitulation. Prussian soldiers, wearing parade uniforms, marched on the squares of Paris as bands played patriotic German songs. But Paris was suspiciously quiet – all windows closed, curtains drawn, not a single spectator in the streets. After two days of celebrations the Germans left Paris – again, with military bands and banners flying. Right away the city was struck with riots – the German parade was the last straw. Parisians turned against the French army and murdered two generals. The government fled to Versailles. Socialist revolutionaries took control of the city, raised the red banner, and proclaimed Paris a socialist city-state – the *Paris Commune*.

The Paris Commune lasted 71 days. Its slogan was "Death to the rich, the land owners, and the priests!" While defending Paris from the German and French armies, the 'communards' went after their enemies in the city as well. They shut down newspapers. Criticizing the revolution was now a crime punishable by death. They also banned religion and private property. Marriage was replaced with so-called 'free love' – a couple didn't have to stay together for more than a day. 70 priests, bishops, and nuns who protested this were first taken hostage, and then stripped naked, humiliated, and executed by the Paris Commune government. The 'communards' ordered all citizens of Paris between 19 and 40 years old to join them under penalty of death. 1200 citizens refused and were executed. Their bodies were mocked and cut into pieces.

"Wilhelm I is proclaimed German Emperor in Versailles Hall of Mirrors" by Anton von Werner

Tuileries Palace burning during the Paris Commune

The American *New York Times* reporter wrote from Paris, "No man who is a man can stand by and see women shot, and children from ten to fourteen years of age put to death, and approve of this. Allowing that, the leaders of the Commune have been guilty of terrible, revolting crimes... At the Luxembourg gardens, there are large trenches filled to the brink with human bodies, many of them only half-killed. Men and women, with hands tied behind their backs, are taken to the brink. There come musket shots, the smoke clears away, and the victims are in the trenches. Horror, horror!..The little garden of the Tour St. Jacques on the Sevastopol Boulevard was a mass of dead bodies, awaiting burial. The barricades in the vicinity were also in a dreadful state, from the dead bodies, half covered, lying all over. Over a thousand are already buried there. Large trenches are dug, and twenty bodies thrown into each trench. Yesterday, near Mr. Washburne's house, 6 children, between the ages of 8 and 10, taken in the act of setting fire to houses, were shot on the spot by an officer of high rank."

The revolutionaries destroyed the Vandome column and set on fire the Cathedral of Notre Dame, the court, and government buildings. They robbed churches and renamed streets. Government troops managed to save the Louvre Palace with its vast treasury of art, but Tuillieries Palace was destroyed. To make sure that the buildings burned all the way to the ground, the communards sent out the 'keroseners' – women and kids who carried buckets of kerosene and poured it around churches and palace halls to be set on fire. Just like the French Revolution of 1789, the Paris Commune targeted churches and Christianity. Cathedrals were plundered, the statues of saints were covered with insulting graffiti. Revolutionaries played cards and got drunk on the church altars. In the church of Saint Eustache, the statue of Virgin Mary was dressed up as a dancer, and *feminists* gathered around it to proclaim women's rights. "Marriage is the greatest error of ancient humanity. To be married is to be a slave!" they shouted.

Outside of Paris, in Versailles, Bismarck helped the anti-revolution French forces form a new government of the Third Republic, the Versailles Assembly. The Prussian army withdrew, and the Assembly was left to handle the Paris Commune. Now it was the Assembly army of around 200,000 besieging Paris defended by a revolutionary army of about the same size – in a tragic civil-war conflict. In the end, Paris fell and 20,000 revolutionaries of the Paris Commune were executed. Germany made France pay five billion francs in reparations (compensation) for the war which added to the suffering of war-torn France and gave rise to the *revanchist* movement (from the French *revanche* = 'revenge') with the focus on re-gaining the international prestige of France.

The new German empire changed the balance of power in Europe. Surprisingly, it tilted Europe toward peace, at least temporarily. German nationalists viewed Russia as a threat and believed that sooner or later a war with Russia was inevitable. Bismarck disagreed. As early as 1863 he wrote, "The secret of politics? Make a good treaty with Russia." His critics labeled him a 'Russian agent' and demanded a 'preemptive war' ('preemptive' = aimed to prevent something) on Russia. But, remembering the fiasco (disaster) Napoleon I suffered in Russia, Bismarck rejected that idea. "Preemptive war is like committing suicide for fear of death," he commented.

To strengthen the empire, Bismarck, nicknamed the 'Iron Chancellor,' promoted 'germanization' – bringing German language and culture to non-German areas under Prussian control – Danish, French, Polish, and other territories captured by Prussia.

Destruction of the Vendôme Colonne during the Paris Commune

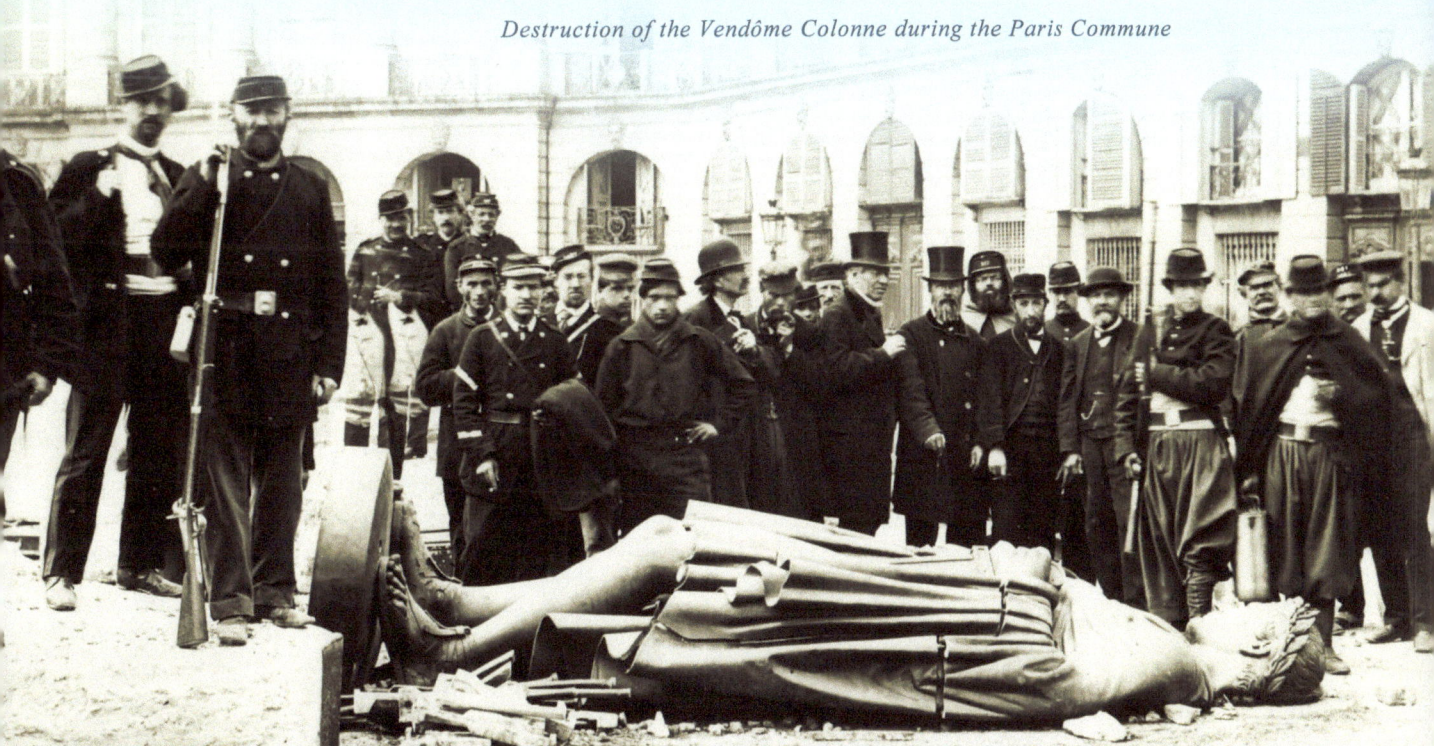

He also sought to reduce the influence of the Catholic church with a policy known as ***Kulturkampf*** (Culture Struggle, or Culture War), promoting anti-Catholic laws. Priests were prohibited to express political opinions during sermons, all appointments of bishops had to be confirmed by the government, religious education had to include science, and civil registration of marriage was made obligatory. The German government withdrew financial support from the Catholic Church and diplomatic relations with the Vatican were broken.

These radical steps did not add to Bismarck's popularity in Prussia, 1/3 of whose population was Catholic. One day a Catholic cardinal who was a Papal Legate (Pope's ambassador) in Prussia, ran into Bismarck in the hallway of a government building. Bismarck wanted to pass him, but the cardinal didn't step aside fast enough, so Bismarck pushed him out of the way. The cardinal looked at Bismarck with indignation. "You don't seem to know who I am," snapped Bismarck. "I am Bismarck." "I see," responded the cardinal. "If that is not an apology, it's at least a perfect explanation."

Polish people – Catholic and divided between Prussia, Austria, and Russia since the end of the 18th century – were a constant target of Bismarck's germanization and Kulturkampf attacks. "Hammer the Poles until they despair of living," he wrote. "I have all the sympathy in the world for their situation, but if we want to exist we have no choice but to wipe them out. Wolves were also created by God, but we shoot them all the same."

Another target of Bismarck's government was the growing socialist movement in Germany. His anti-socialist laws banned trade unions, socialist organizations and rallies, socialist literature and newspapers. Predictably, these measures had an opposite effect, and the German Social Democratic Party was only growing and getting more and more seats in the Reichstag. Following his Realpolitik principles, Bismarck decided to undermine the socialist movement by taking their ideas and having the German government implement them. This resulted in reforms that offered benefits for the elderly, sickness and injury insurance, and inexpensive medical care for all citizens. It's likely that Bismarck was the first to come up with the idea of a pension – government payments to older people who retire from work. In 1889 Germany started providing assistance to people over the age of 70.

Like other European empires, Germany was in the race to capture as many colonies as possible to use the natural resources and labor of the colonized lands for the benefit of the German economy. At first Bismarck believed that colonies didn't "pay for themselves," because "tropical people" were "incapable" of maintaining order and productivity. However, in the 1880s, as Britain and France imported massive quantities of exotic goods and products from their colonies, not having colonies became equal to losing international prestige. So Bismarck sent German troops to Africa to compete with France and Britain in what became known as the *Scramble for Africa*. German colonies included parts of the present day Togo, Ghana, Cameroon, Nigeria, Rwanda, Burundi, Tanzania, and Namibia. In the Pacific Germany captured the Northeastern part of New Guinea.

In 1888, Kaiser Wilhelm I died. His grandson, Wilhelm II became the Kaiser of the German Empire. He wanted a more aggressive policy in Europe, while Bismarck was done with wars. Interestingly, in 1888 Bismarck even predicted World War I. "One day the great European War will come out of some damned foolish thing in the Balkans," he wrote. Eventually, Bismarck's conflict with the new Kaiser resulted in his resignation in 1890. He spent his last years writing memoirs and died in 1898, at the age of 83.

Bismarck was rumored to like only the English, Americans, and Russians. But whether a nation had his respect or not, Bismarck managed to say something insulting about everyone! Here is a selection of insulting quotes by Bismarck.

About Russians: Never believe Russians, because even they, themselves, don't believe themselves. Never plot against Russia. For any strategic move you make, they'll respond with something entirely unpredictable – their stupidity.
About Americans: God always looks after fools, drunks, kids, and the United States of America. Americans are very lucky people. In the north and south their neighbors are weak nations, and in the east and west it's fish.
About Poles: You can't destroy Poles on the battlefield, but if you give them power, they will destroy themselves.
About Bavarian Germans: A Bavarian is half-way between an Austrian and a human being.
About journalists: A journalist is a person who has mistaken their calling.
About fools: Only a fool learns from his own mistakes. The wise man learns from the mistakes of others.

Alexander II
1818 – 1881

While revolutions were shaking Europe, and European monarchies adopted constitutions and worked out the balance between more freedoms and fewer riots, the Russian Empire remained an absolute monarchy throughout the 19th century. The tsars of the Romanov dynasty didn't see the need to modernize the country and the system of government. Most changes they introduced were half-hearted, while the revolutionary movements in Russia were gaining strength throughout the Victorian era.

The Crimean War (1854 – 1856) was a painful defeat for Russia. It undermined the – already fading – faith in the monarchy among the Russian public. From inside Russia, Tsar Nicholas I and his advisors looked like a bunch of talentless amateurs. Unfortunately for the country, this image wasn't far from reality. The age of daring Russian monarchs, such as Peter the Great or Catherine the Great, was long gone. Devastated by the defeat in the Crimean War, Nicholas I died in 1855 – officially from illness, but actually from heartbreak. His son, the new Russian Emperor Alexander II, needed to act fast to restore the prestige of the Russian throne inside the country and internationally. He needed reforms, since the Russian public blamed the defeat in the war on the backwardness of the Russian economy and social order.

Alexander received the typical education of a Russian noble of that era. The subjects he studied as a kid included the Russian language and literature, history, geography, statistics, law, economics, finance, ethnography, logic, philosophy, mathematics, physics, mineralogy, geology, drawing, music, gymnastics, fencing, swimming, dancing, public speaking, military arts, and Bible studies. Alexander was given tests twice a year in the presence of his dad, Nicholas I. He spoke French, German, English, and Polish. At age 20 he completed his education and was taken on a tour of Russia, visiting 29 provinces of his future empire. The next year his parents sent him to tour Western Europe. The European tour was a standard element of the education of the Russian nobility, but in the case of Alexander, an additional goal was to find him a bride. His parents allowed him to make his own choice as long as the bride was not Catholic.

In London Alexander met 20-year-old Queen Victoria. The rumor was... they fell in love! They spent 3 days together, holding hands and behaving like they'd known each other for years. Victoria wrote in her diary, "I am totally in love with the prince. He is so adorable, such a nice, handsome guy." But marriage between the Queen of England and the future Emperor of Russia was out of the question. Husbands and wives of kings and queens were to be chosen from aristocratic families that had no power – to prevent in-laws from influencing the monarchs. Victoria was politely asked to stop flirting with the Russian and go home. Alexander's parents were in panic, and the prince was ordered to leave England at once. He left for Germany.

In Darmstadt he met 14-year-old German princess, Marie of Hesse, and decided to propose marriage to her. Alexander's parents objected, thinking she was not royal enough, but Alexander was done with their advice. Two years later, when Marie was 16, she was engaged to Alexander, and a year later they got married.

Empress Marie by Franz Winterhalter

In the mid-19th century the Russian Empire included many provinces that used to be sovereign countries, but lost wars and ended up becoming part of Russia – Poland, Finland, Latvia, Lithuania, and Estonia in Europe, Georgia, Armenia, and Azerbaijan in the Caucasus... These also included territories chopped off of other ancient empires, such as vast areas of Central Asia and the Far East, as well as lands claimed by Russian explorers, like Alaska. The economy and social situation in each province was different, ranging from European-style economies in the West, to completely medieval provinces in Central Asia and the Caucasus. But it was the largest portion of the empire, Russia itself, that was its weakest link. Its cities were going through an industrial revolution. Mining, metallurgy, a weapons industry, consumer goods factories, and railroads were growing, while in the countryside life didn't differ much from that of the Middle Ages.

Of the 47 million peasants who lived in rural Russia, more than half worked on lands that belonged to the 'crown' – to the Russian state or to Russian Orthodox monasteries. Their villages enjoyed self-government, had their own local courts with judge and jury, and various privileges. However, a little less than half, 21 million, lived on lands that belonged to private landowners. These people were bound by the Russian Law Code of 1649 that prohibited them from leaving the land where they worked and virtually made them the physical property of their owners, a status close to that of a slave. These peasants – or 'serfs' – could be sold by their owners, just like slaves, could be punished by their landlords without trial or police involvement. These were the poorest citizens of the Russian empire, and the Russian public demanded that these serfs be freed – and compensated for two centuries of forced labor by letting them own the land on which they worked.

So, as one of his first and most radical reforms, Alexander II issued a 'freedom manifesto' and a royal decree releasing the serfs from any obligations to their land owners. He took steps to compensate the land owners for potential loss of the serfs' labor. He also bought 350 million acres of land from the landowners to make more self-governed, independent, 'crown' villages, giving peasants 50 years to pay for it. However, the peasants didn't understand why they should pay for land on which their families had lived forever. This resulted in riots. Russian upper classes and educated professionals – the *intelligentsia* – approved of Alexander's reforms, but believed they were not enough. Some wanted parliamentary constitutional monarchy, others fell under the influence of socialist ideas spreading like wildfire in France and Germany, and sought to import the European revolutionary movements into Russia. While in Germany and other more industrial countries revolutionary movements were led by socialists and focused on the rights of industrial workers, in Russia the class of industrial workers was smaller and uninterested in revolution. So Russian revolutionaries embraced philosophies of protest, such as *nihilism* and *anarchism*, combined with the tactics of terrorism.

Nihilism

Nihilism as a philosophy states that life has no meaning, and that it's impossible to gain any real knowledge of the world and of human nature. It also rejects all religious and moral principles. However, as a revolutionary movement that emerged in the 1850s, Russian nihilism focused on extreme moral and social skepticism, denying and undermining existing personal and social values, such as Christian faith, family ties, the relationship between man and woman, social order. It also rejected monarchy as the basis of the Russian political system.

Russian silver tea pot, 19th century

Anarchism

Anarchism is a political philosophy that rejects any form of authority and seeks to destroy any institutions that claim authority over people, such as governments or churches.

Intelligentsia

The term 'intelligentsia' was coined in Poland in the 19th century. It referred to a class of university-educated professionals performing intellectual labor, such as scholars, teachers, journalists, and writers. The term became popular in Russia where it acquired a broader meaning – intellectually-active citizens who either engage in developing cultural and political trends or enjoy intellectual and cultural products – literature, art, theater.

In 1864 a Russian revolutionary named Mikhail Bakunin escaped from **Siberia** where he had been exiled for spreading anti-monarchy views, settled in London, and started publishing the *Kolokol* ('Bell' in Russian) anarchist paper. The Kolokol was smuggled into Russia and read by thousands of university students and intellectuals seeking social reforms. Many young people formed secret societies teaching nihilism and anarchism and worked on strategies to strike the monarchy through acts of individual terrorism – assassinations. One of these societies, **The People's Will**, was convinced that if the Tsar were to be assassinated, the result would be a mass uprising of the peasants that would spearhead the revolution. These **radical** (extremist) groups acted with confidence because they had the secret support of wide circles of the Russian liberal intelligentsia and the press. Alexander's advisors had no idea how to curb the spreading of the revolutionary moods. The Minister of Education made Latin and Greek, as well as a lot of heavy-duty math, obligatory in the curriculum of all schools. He thought maybe if kids were busy with subjects that required a lot of focus, they would stop reading socialist newspapers smuggled from Europe. Needless to say, this initiative failed to keep young Russians from opposing the monarchy.

Left: Traditional Russian peasant shirt

Next page: A map of European Russia (West of the Ural Mountains), 1890. Russian European provinces included Great Russia (Central Russia), Finland, Baltic provinces (Latvia, Lithuania, Estonia), Poland, West Russia (includes present-day Belarus), Little Russia (present-day Ukraine*), South Russia (Black Sea Coast) & the Caucasus (present-day Armenia, Georgia, Azerbaijan & more).

* 'Ukraine' (Украина) means 'periphery, edge, outskirts' in Russian. Up to the 20th century, 'Ukraine' was used to refer to the Western 'edge' of Russia, the borderlands between Russia and Poland.

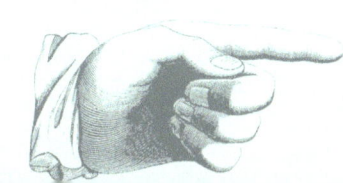

Poland – governed by Russia, with a 'territory' status similar to a colony, was another source of headaches for Alexander II. The Poles asked for self-government, but Alexander refused to grant it. Nationalist moods in Poland were stronger than ever, and secret societies operated by Polish exiles in Europe spread socialist ideas among Polish workers and peasants. Alexander was afraid of a Polish revolution and a war with Austria and Prussia, who also owned chunks of Poland since its 2nd Division in the 18th century. In 1863, an uprising broke out in Warsaw. It was led by Polish socialists, followers of Karl Marx. Russian troops crushed it. Its leaders were executed. Poland lost its 'territory' status and was made a regular province of Russia.

Siberia

Siberia is North Asia, from the Ural Mountains (that separate Europe from Asia) to the Pacific Ocean. Between the 16th and 18th centuries Russia conquered a few native kingdoms in Siberia and it became part of Russia. Because of its harsh climate, up to the mid-19th century Siberia remained mostly uninhabited. As its vast natural resources were being discovered, people started migrating there from European Russia. In the 17th century, the Russian government established penal labor colonies in Siberia, sending convicted criminals to work in Siberian mines. It was a system similar to 'penal transportation' in Britain (sending convicted criminals to remote colonies, such as Australia). The Russian imperial justice system also exiled political dissidents (members of the political opposition) and their families to Siberia.

The 'Polish events' turned both Polish and Russian liberal intelligentsia against Alexander II. In 1866 an unemployed university dropout with a history of suicide attempts was recruited by a revolutionary group in Moscow. In April 1866 he came armed to the Summer Garden public park in St.Petersburg. Everybody knew that every day Alexander II walked his favorite dog, an Irish setter named Milord, in the park. Kids loved the royal dog and many families stopped by to see the emperor and his pet. There was even a joke that the emperor (who usually wore a nondescript military uniform) could be recognized by his dog. The would-be assassin fired a gun at the Tsar at the gates of the park. Alexander was saved by a guy in the crowd of onlookers who noticed the gun in the assassin's hand and pushed him right before he fired. The assassin was seized.

Entrance to the Summer Garden and the would-be assassin Dmitry Karakozov

The tsar came up to meet him and asked, "Are you Polish?" "No," answered the assassin. "Then what do you want?" "Nothing, nothing," mumbled the revolutionary. He faced trial and was executed. 26 members of his revolutionary cell received prison terms. Next year, as Alexander II was visiting the 1867 World's Fair in Paris, a Polish immigrant fired a gun at the carriage that took Alexander and Napoleon III to the exhibition. The gun misfired.

In 1867 Alexander made another unpopular move. He decided that it was not realistic to defend 'Russian America,' Alaska, in case of a war – and sold Alaska to the United States for $7.2 million (equivalent to $151 million in 2022). He described it as a gesture of good will. Alexander was a fan of the USA, cultivated friendship with American politicians, and supported the Union during the American Civil War. Russia even sent its battleships to New York and San Francisco to guard their harbors against the Confederate Navy.

Alaska purchase US Treasury warrant (the check with which the US bought Alaska)

Alexander was criticized not only for his political decisions, but also for his personal life. By the 1860s he and his wife, Empress Marie, had 8 kids – 6 sons and 2 daughters. But Alexander cheated on his wife with her ladies-in-waiting and pretty actresses, and the reports of his adventures caused scandals. Marie suffered from tuberculosis, and in 1866 her condition worsened. She suggested to Alexander a secret separation agreement, and he started courting a young Russian aristocrat Catherine Dolgorukova. Catherine agreed to a relationship with the tsar on the condition that he would be faithful to her, and that she should be treated like his wife. Alexander promised her that if Empress Marie died before him, he would marry Catherine. The royal children couldn't stand Catherine and stopped talking to their dad. Catherine and Alexander had 3 kids. Alexander's advisors and ministers suspected that Catherine, who was liberal in her political views, was trying to persuade the emperor to introduce a constitution.

Princess Ekaterina (Catherine) Dolgorukova

It's likely that they were right, because in one of his letters to her, Alexander wrote, "As far as a constitution is concerned, as long as I live, I won't agree to it, and won't let anyone impose it on me, and enough talking about this."

In 1876 an anti-Turkish revolt broke out in Bulgaria that had been occupied by the Ottoman Empire for over 400 years. Suppressing the revolt, the Turkish army massacred 20 thousand Bulgarians. Sympathy for Bulgaria – an Orthodox Christian nation, like Russia – united all classes of Russian society, and all political groups, from liberals to monarchists. Thousands of Russians volunteered to help liberate Bulgaria. It was a great opportunity for Emperor Alexander to improve his image in the eyes of the Russian public and restore the losses of the Crimean War. In 1877 Alexander's government led a coalition of Balkan principalities (princedoms), including Bulgaria, Romania, Serbia, and Montenegro against the Ottoman Turkish Empire. Russia won the war, but the casualties were staggering. 30 thousand Russian soldiers were killed, plus over 80 thousand died from wounds and disease. The Ottoman losses were about the same. The Turkish army and its commander Osman Pasha surrendered, and Bulgaria was liberated after the 480-year rule of the Ottoman Empire.

The last chapter of the war was the **Battle of the Shipka Pass**. The Russian army and the Bulgarian volunteer troops led by Russian general Skobelev crossed the Balkan Mountains in the middle of a massive snowstorm and defeated the Turkish forces in a narrow mountain pass, capturing 36 thousand men and 90 guns. To prevent the Russians from taking Constantinople, the British Empire sent its fleet to block it. Remember the *Jingo* song?
...We've fought the Bear before, and while we're Britons true
    The Russians shall not have Constantinople!

"General Skobelev greets the troops after the Russian victory at the Shipka Pass" by Vasily Vereshchagin

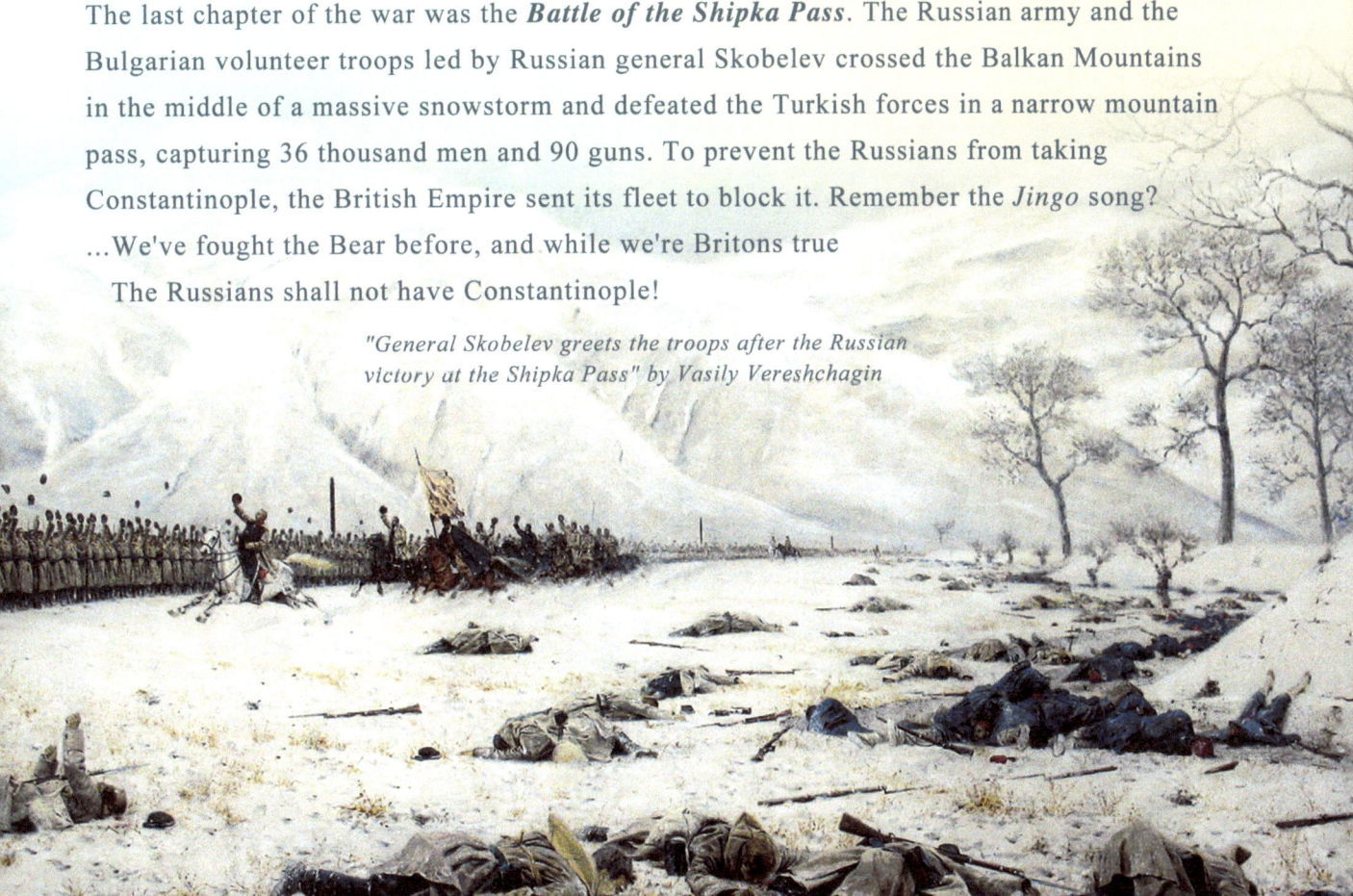

At this point Alexander II believed he had achieved some popularity and no further reforms were necessary. He was proud of his nickname – the 'Tsar Liberator.' In addition to releasing Russian peasants from serfdom, he also freed Bulgaria and other Balkan Christians from the Turks. But his subjects disagreed. As the war wound down, the rumors of horrific losses and the realization that the war brought hardly any gain for Russia, pushed the Russian public opinion from rooting for the Russian troops to condemning the war. Many chalked it up as another failure of Alexander II. The horrors of the Russo-Turkish war were captured in spectacular paintings of the famous 19th century Russian artist Vasily Vereshchagin. His portrayal of the war was so graphic that his paintings were banned in Germany, Austria, and in Russia (where the ban also extended to reproductions of his paintings in books and magazines).

In 1877 Russian police arrested 253 nihilists. 160 of them were convicted. One of the convicts refused to take off his hat in the presence of Colonel Trepov, Governor of St.Petersburg. Trepov ordered prison guards to beat him up. This incident outraged both the revolutionaries and the liberal intelligentsia.

Above: "The Apotheosis of War" by Vasily Vereshchagin;
Left: "Russian troops enter Tyrnovo, Bolgaria" by Nikolai Dmitriev-Orenburgsky

The newspapers were openly calling for revenge, and Trepov was 'sentenced to death' by a mysterious 'executive committee' – one of the anarchist terrorist cells. Soon a member of that cell, Polish noblewoman Vera Zasulich, shot and wounded Trepov. The judge at her trial was a prominent liberal intellectual who allowed defense witnesses to testify against Trepov's unjustified cruelty. The sympathy of the jury was entirely on the side of Vera Zasulich and she was acquitted. The Russian public praised the justice system that was able to 'stand up to the authorities.' Actually, they had Alexander II to thank for it. It was his judicial reform of 1864 that made the jury and defense by a professional attorney obligatory in criminal trials in Russia. But the educated public despised Alexander, and the revolutionaries concluded that using terrorism to force social change worked superbly well.

Vera Zasulich

And so, a 'reign of terror' began, with assassination attempts happening right and left. Anarchists provoked panic by first 'warning' their future victim of their sentence. Notes announcing the future assassination and signed "Executive Committee," were delivered to newspaper offices or nailed to the door of the victims' houses. In Kiev, the Malorossia ('Little Russia') province of Russia, the president of the local university was shot and wounded, and a police officer was stabbed. Next, the Chief of the Russian Secret Police was killed in St.Petersburg, the Governor of Kharkov (Malorossia) was wounded, and the Police chief of Odessa in the province of South Russia was killed. Terrorists set government and police buildings on fire in Moscow and other cities, and incited riots. In 1878, the government proclaimed martial law, and appointed the most experienced Russian generals as governors of the troublesome provinces. A Supreme Executive Commission was formed to fight the revolutionaries. Dozens of revolutionaries were imprisoned, executed, or exiled to Siberia.

In April of 1879, as Alexander was strolling on the grounds of the Winter Palace (the royal residence in St.Petersburg), another unemployed university dropout (and revolutionary terrorist) approached him with gun in hand. Until this assassination attempt, Alexander, like his dad Nicholas I, had never employed bodyguards. When Alexander saw the gun, he started running in a zigzag pattern, using the sniper evasion technique he learned as part of his military training. The assassin fired 5 times and missed. He was sentenced to death and executed a month later. But the revolutionaries didn't give up.

In December of 1879 Alexander arrived in Moscow by train. As the train was pulling into the station, a mine planted by the People's Will revolutionary group blew up one of the train cars. Alexander happened to be in another car. Three days later Moscow residents started finding flyers announcing that the emperor had been sentenced to death by an 'Executive Committee.' The hunt was on for real now. Alexander's cold-blooded reaction to all these assassination attempts surprised both his contemporaries and biographers. He never panicked, and never felt anger toward the revolutionaries who tried to take his life. He was a fatalist, like many royals before him, but people wanted a more intriguing explanation. One of the legends that 'explained' Alexander's courage went like this: A famous gypsy fortune teller told the tsar that he would survive 7 assassination attempts. However, she failed to indicate whether there would be an 8th attempt...

In February 1880, an explosive device went off in the guard room of the Winter Palace. The room was located a story below and directly underneath the imperial dining room. 11 guards were killed, but Alexander survived: He was late for dinner that day...

Fatalism

Fatalism is the belief in 'fate' or 'destiny,' the idea that the course of human life is predestined – determined by each person's fate/destiny – and doesn't depend on our decisions and actions. 'Fate' comes from the Latin noun 'fatum' – 'prediction.' The literal meaning of 'fatum' is 'what is said/predicted' (from the verb 'fari' – to speak).

Interiors of the Winter Palace, the residence of the royal Romanov family in St.Petersburg, Russia

In addition to panic, a scandal erupted in the palace. When Alexander heard the explosion, he ran to the third floor shouting "Katia, my dearest Katia!" 'Katia' is a diminutive (affectionate) form of the Russian name Ekaterina = Catherine. He was concerned that Catherine Dolgorukova, who lived in a private apartment on the third floor, might have been injured. Courtiers and Alexander's kids couldn't believe he was worrying about Catherine and never even inquired about Empress Marie who might have been injured as well. By that time Marie was very sick with tuberculosis and later that year she died. On her deathbed she asked to meet the kids her husband had with Catherine. Alexander brought Catherine's son and daughter to see Marie, and Marie blessed them. Soon after Marie's funeral, Alexander fulfilled his promise to Catherine and married her in a secret ceremony at the Royal Village Palace near St.Petersburg. This marriage was extremely unpopular with the Russian public, and Alexander's older kids were furious. Catherine, in her turn, despised them, calling them 'heartless, uneducated monsters.'

Soon after the explosion in the Winter Palace, the nihilists published a proclamation saying that the tsar would be left alone if he agreed to establish a constitutional monarchy. Alexander's top advisors suggested that maybe the tsar should indeed take some steps to reconcile with the revolutionaries. Alexander agreed. He pardoned many political prisoners (including assassins sentenced to death), and ordered 2,000 students expelled from the universities for revolutionary activity to be readmitted. The Council of State started discussing a constitution and worked out a step-by-step plan of liberalization for Russia. Alexander approved the plan and signed it into law on March 13, 1881. That same day, as his carriage was on its way to the Winter Palace, an assassin threw a bomb under the carriage wheels. A few guards were injured. The tsar rushed to help the wounded. At that moment another bomb exploded right next to him. The tsar died from the wounds later that afternoon.

"Assassination of Alexander II" by M.P. Silayev

The police arrested the assassin, a People's Will member, but rumors persisted that the assassination was ordered by those close to the throne - monarchists who were opposed to constitutional government.

After Alexander's death, the royal family hinted to Catherine that she should get lost. She and her kids were not allowed inside the cathedral where Alexander's funeral mass took place, and had to stand in the doorway. Catherine was given a very generous pension and moved to Paris where she became a celebrity and a fashion icon. She died in 1922.

Alexander's son, Alexander III, inherited the Russian throne. He didn't want to hear about a constitution or reforms. Alexander III focused on hunting down Russian revolutionary organizations. As a result of his policy, the politically-active layers of Russian society, led by the liberal intelligentsia, began to side with the radical revolutionaries. The chance for peaceful reforms was lost. When Alexander II was murdered, Vladimir Lenin – the future leader of the 1917 Socialist revolution in Russia – was 11 years old. A new generation of revolutionaries was not going to settle for peanuts like constitutional monarchy.
Russia was turning into a time bomb, and the clock was ticking.
It was 1881 – only 24 years until the first Russian revolution (1905)...
and only 36 years until 1917...

Alexander III, Vladiir Lenin in 1887, and the Church of Our Savior on the Spilled Blood in St.Petersburg built on the spot of Alexander II's assassination

Giuseppe Garibaldi
1807 – 1882

In the early 19th century, Italy – just like Germany – was made of many kingdoms, dukedoms, principalities, and city states. The north of Italy was dominated by Austria. The largest country in the south was the Kingdom of the Two Sicilies. In the middle were the Papal States, ruled by the pope. The unification of Italy started with the small kingdom of Piedmont-Sardinia whose territory was the island of Sardinia in the Mediterranean and a small piece of 'mainland' Italy. The king of Piedmont-Sardinia, Vittorio Emanuele II, appointed Count Camillo di Cavour (1810-1861), as the head of his government. Historians consider Cavour 'the architect' of Italian unification. Cavour – a fan of Bismarck's Realpolitik – made a deal with Napoleon III. In exchange for the city of Nice, which was given to France, Piedmont-Sardinia received French military support and pushed the Austrians out of northern Italy in 1859. But what about the South? Adding it to the unified Kingdom of Italy was carried out by Giuseppe Garibaldi. Interestingly, he was a native of Nice...

Garibaldi was an adventurer who spent most of his life as a mercenary soldier fighting on the side of the native rebels in uprisings and wars of independence, mostly in South America. Garibaldi grew up on the seashore. His dad, the owner of a small merchant ship, took him on voyages to Rome and Constantinople. As a kid Garibaldi disliked school and missed as many classes as he could get away with. One of his childhood friends wrote in his memoir: "He missed school whenever he could come up with an adventure – talk a grownup to let him shoot a gun, or take him on a boat trip, or oyster-trawling... but he was often thoughtful and silent, and when he had a book that interested him, he would lie under the olive-trees for hours reading... He had a beautiful voice, and knew all the songs of the peasants and sailors, and a good many French ones besides. Even as a boy we all looked up to him, while the little ones regarded him as their protector."

Italian cavalry sword, 19th century;
Italian tea pot, Egyptian Revival style

When Garibaldi was 15, his dad gave up on his son's education and started training him as a merchant ship captain. In 1833 he took a shipment of oranges from Italy to the Russian town of Taganrog on the Sea of Azov. Over there, at the port, he met some Italians who were members of the nationalist *Young Italy* secret society organized by Giuseppe Mazzini, a lifelong fighter for Italian unification.

Above: The Carbonari's initiation ritual, held in a cave; Below: Freemasons secret initiation ritual

This was the defining moment in Garibaldi's life. He joined the Italian Carbonari – a network of secret societies fighting for Italian independence and unification. The Carbonari were an offshoot of French Masonry. In the 18th and 19th centuries Masonic lodges of Europe and America spread the ideas of the French Revolution, enabled revolutionaries to network, and nurtured anti-Catholic movements. Along with the members of his Carbonari 'cell,' Garibaldi joined an armed revolt organized by Mazzini in Piedmont. The revolt failed, Garibaldi was sentenced to death, and fled to France.

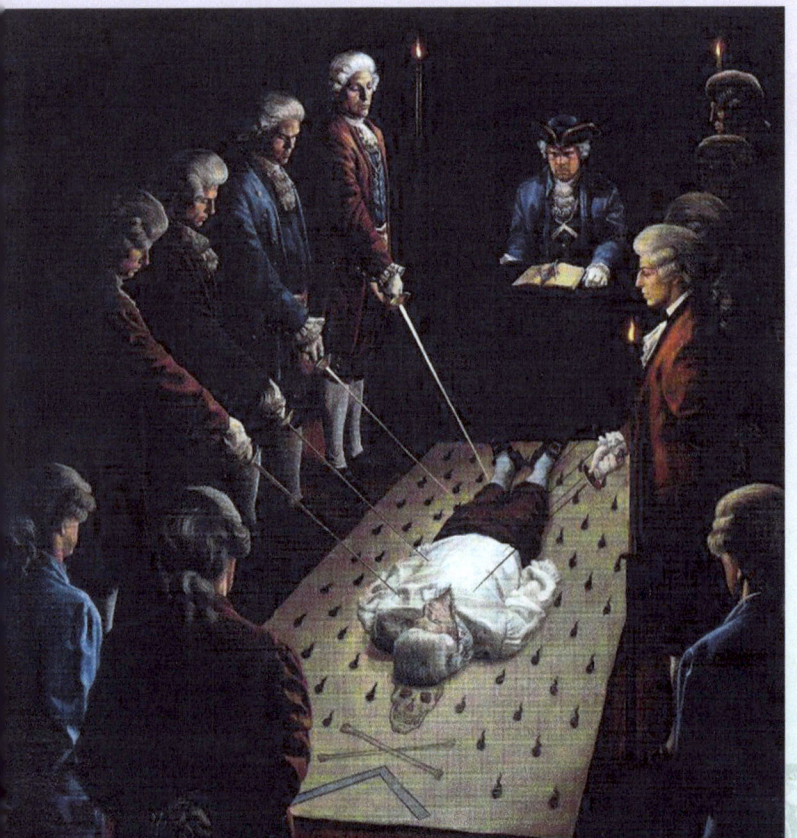

Masonry

Masons, or Freemasons, were organizations that emerged in the 14th century in Europe as guilds – or labor unions – of stone workers – masons. While some of these organizations (also referred to as Masonic lodges) stayed away from political life and focused on networking and charity causes, others became centers of revolutionary political activity. Most thinkers of the Enlightenment era, and leaders of the revolutionary movements in Europe, such as Rousseau, Voltaire, Robespierre, and Garibaldi were Freemasons. To join a Masonic lodge, members went through a secret initiation ceremony to be later promoted from the lowest 'degree' of an apprentice to the highest 'degree' of a Master Mason. Members of the lodges used secret signs and words to recognize fellow masons. They accepted faith in God, but discouraged religious activity within the masonic movement.

Carbonari and 'Alta Vendita'

The Carbonari secret societies operated in Italy in the early 19th century. Along with fighting for Italian independence and unification, Carbonari also sought to replace European monarchies with republics. The term carbonari – "charcoal-burners" – referred to the charcoal trade. Similar to masons (stone workers), Carbonari traced their origin to coal trade guilds. Their secret ceremonies were fashioned after masonic rites. They called their meeting places 'barracks.' Members of their secret cells were referred to as 'good cousins.' Carbonari fought against the Pope and the Papal States, and many of them rejected Catholicism. The Carbonari of Sicily were rumored to have authored a controversial document, **Alta Vendita** *(Italian for 'The High Market Place') published in the early 1800s. Alta Vendita called for the masonic infiltration of the Catholic Church in order to destroy it from inside. It suggested that as the anti-religious ideas of the French Revolution spread around, some masons and revolution sympathizers would eventually become priests and cardinals. At some point, a pope would be elected from their ranks, and the liberal takeover of the church would be complete.*

Ragamuffins

Anita Garibaldi

From France, Garibaldi sailed to Brazil, where he joined a Brazilian rebel group named the **Ragamuffins**. The Ragamuffins were 'separatists' – fighters for the separation of the southern Brazilian province of Rio Grande do Sul from the Brazilian Empire (which had, in its turn, declared independence from Portugal in 1822). They were nicknamed 'ragamuffins' (Portuguese: *farrapos*) after the leather fringe on the clothes of the *gauchos* – Latin American cowboys. While fighting in the **Ragamuffin Wars**, Garibaldi met his future wife Anita (her full name was Ana Maria de Jesus Ribeiro da Silva). In his memoirs Garibaldi describes meeting Anita. Standing on the deck of a captured Brazilian battleship, "I cast my eyes toward the houses on the south side of the lagoon and saw a young woman. Right away I gave orders to get the boat ready...I came ashore, and, when I had just given up hope of seeing her again, I ran into an acquaintance who invited me for coffee at his place. When we walked into his house, the first person who met my eyes was the girl I saw on the shore..."

"...We both remained stunned and silent, looking at each other as if seeking in each other's faces something from the forgotten past. I spoke very little Portuguese, so I said in Italian, 'Tu devi essere mia' – 'You must be mine.'
That was a tie, a decree, which death alone could break."

Ragamuffin / gaucho

Anita was a Brazilian revolutionary. She married Garibaldi, and together they fought in the Ragamuffin troops. One day the Ragamuffins lost a battle. Anita was captured by the enemy and told that her husband had been killed. She asked permission to go look for him on the battlefield, but didn't find him among the fallen fighters. As the night came, her guards got drunk. Anita stole one of their horses and escaped. The enemy posts let her through. She was so beautiful and rode so fast, they thought she was a ghost.

Anita and Garibaldi also fought in the Uruguayan Civil Wars – as part of an Italian Legion that Garibaldi organized. There were a lot of Italians living in Uruguay. That's where Garibaldi started wearing gaucho clothes – the red woolen shirt, poncho, and sombrero – that became the trademark of his troops. The wars were brutal. Garibaldi was tired of never-ending hostilities, so one day he gave up the soldier's life and became a math teacher in Montevideo, the capital of Uruguay. Garibaldi and Anita had 4 kids. The Uruguay government offered to reward Garibaldi with land and a high military rank, but Garibaldi declined. He didn't want to owe anything to any government. As a result, his family lived in near-poverty. One day Anita discovered that a few coins, her last savings, were missing. Her husband confessed that he had taken them to buy a doll for their little daughter. Garibaldi visited his military friends only in the daytime, always wearing a poncho, supposedly to protect him from the sun. The real reason was, his clothes were so worn out, he couldn't show up without a poncho.

During the 1848 revolutionary events in Europe, Garibaldi and Anita came to Italy. Garibaldi participated in the ***First Italian War of Independence*** against the Austrian occupation, but the war was lost. Meanwhile, Mazzini and his followers took over Rome, the capital of the Papal States, and proclaimed it a republic. Garibaldi led the Italian volunteers who defended Rome against French troops sent to suppress the rebellion. Pope Pius IX fled and, from exile, excommunicated (denied the rite of communion, as punishment) the rebels, including Garibaldi. Garibaldi wasn't upset. He was already a legend – treated like a great hero by his followers, and nicknamed the 'Red Devil' by his enemies. He always wore his signature red shirt, the 'camicia rossa,' and rode a white horse. Always seen next to him, riding a black horse, was a man nicknamed the Shadow. It was Andrea Aguyar, a former black slave from Uruguay, who had become Garibaldi's right-hand man. Many people in the Papal States supported Garibaldi and the republic. The idea that the authority of the pope was enforced by France, that the papal power rested on the 'foreigners' bayonets,' made people side with the rebels. Whenever French shells burst in the city, Romans angrily exclaimed, "Ecco un Pio Nono!" – 'There goes a Pius IX!'

The defense of Rome ended in a defeat. Aguyar perished. Instead of surrender, Garibaldi chose to lead 4000 fighters out of Rome toward Venice where Italians were still fighting against Austria. "Where we are, there Rome will be," he told the council of his commanders. "Hunger and thirst and vigil I offer you. But we'll never negotiate with the enemy. Whoever loves his country and glory may follow us." However, during Garibaldi's retreat, most of his fighters deserted or were killed. Only 250 remained. Anita died too, and Garibaldi left Italy again.

Below: Garibaldi and Shadow defending Rome
Left: Death of Anita Garibaldi

In 1850 he arrived in New York City, where he was supposed to purchase a ship for a friend of his, a wealthy Italian merchant. Waiting for the purchase to go through, Garibaldi stayed in New York, and even worked at a candle factory on Staten Island. In the following years he worked as a ship captain taking merchant cargo across the Pacific Ocean between China and Peru, and across the Atlantic – to England. In 1854 Garibaldi returned to Italy and received £1400 as an inheritance from his brother who had recently died. On that money he bought half of the island of Caprera near Sardinia and started a farm there.

One of Garibaldi's biographers, Augusto Vittorio Vecchi, who visited Garibaldi's farm, described the search for a new-born lamb who got lost at the farm. Garibaldi, his kids and friends looked for it for hours. Finally, Garibaldi remained the only person who persisted in the search. "It was nine o'clock and raining, and we were very tired, so we returned to the house. About midnight we heard a voice. It was our hero [Garibaldi] returning, joyfully carrying the lost lamb in his arms. He put the little creature in his own bed, and gave it a piece of sponge dipped in milk to suck on, to keep it quiet ... He spent the whole night petting and feeding the foolish little creature! At five in the morning we found him planting potatoes in the garden. We took our spades and began to work also."

When the war between France and Austria began in 1859, Garibaldi fought on the side of France and Piedmont-Sardinia. To his shock, his native town of Nice was given to the French as payment for their support. Then came the most famous episode of Garibaldi's career, the **Expedition of the Thousand**. In May 1860 Garibaldi gathered 800 volunteers – unemployed artisans, professionals, and university students. They were nicknamed 'redshirts,' but they called themselves 'i Mille' – 'the Thousand.' They boarded two beat-up steamships, and headed for Sicily. One of Garibaldi's 19th-century biographers described Sicily in these words, "The kingdom of the Two Sicilies, was, owing to corrupt and tyrannical government, the plague-spot of Europe and the scandal of enlightened Christendom."

Garibaldi's house on Caprera

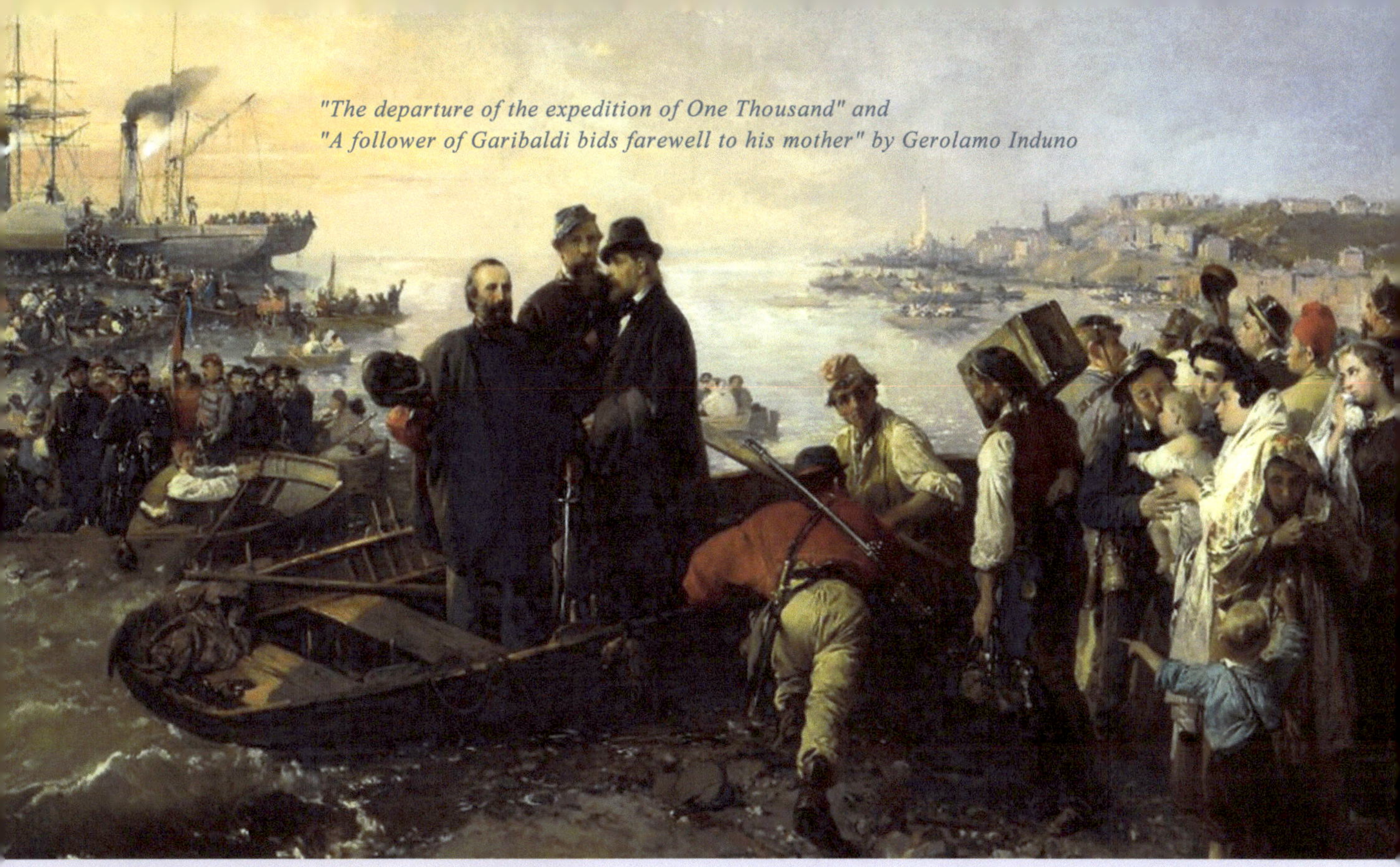

"The departure of the expedition of One Thousand" and
"A follower of Garibaldi bids farewell to his mother" by Gerolamo Induno

"If you join me, you must learn to live without bread and to fight without cartridges," Garibaldi told his men. Indeed, they were short on weapons and ammunition, but they had endless patience, staying for days without food and creeping on narrow goat paths in the mountains to ambush the enemy.
"Here we make Italy or die," these words, said by Garibaldi to his troops, became legendary. In no time Garibaldi's forces captured Palermo, the capital of Sicily, defeating Neapolitan troops. In one of the battles, Garibaldi's son Menotti was wounded. His men asked Garibaldi not to risk his son's life again. "I only wish I had twenty Menottis," answered Garibaldi, "so that I might risk them all."

Sicilian peasants joined Garibaldi, hoping he would abolish taxes, take the land from the landowners and distribute it among the poor.

Above: The siege of Palermo; Below: Garibaldi enters Naples

But Garibaldi wasn't a socialist. He promised the landowners to protect their property, and they joined him too! Most Neapolitan officers were bribed to 'lose' battles. After his victory in Sicily, Garibaldi crossed to mainland Italy and headed to Naples – with a force of 24,000 men. At this point Garibaldi's name opened gates of towns like magic and his redshirts were so famous and so admired in Italy, that small Neapolitan garrisons surrendered without resistance. When Garibaldi entered the city of Naples, the crowds shouted "Viva Garibaldi!" The king of Naples had fled, but the guards by the royal palace didn't know this and prepared for battle. When Garibaldi appeared on the square in front of the palace in an open carriage, the guards pointed their guns at him. But Garibaldi remained calm. He stood up and looked at the soldiers, arms folded on his chest. The 'Viva Garibaldi!' chanting stopped. After a minute, one of the soldiers shouted "Viva Garibaldi!" The guards threw their guns on the ground and joined the crowd of Garibaldi fans.

To protect the Papal States from Garibaldi, Cavour ordered the Sardinian army to occupy the Papal States before Garibaldi's troops arrived. On October 26, 1860, Garibaldi and King Victor Emmanuel II met on a bridge in the town of Teano in Southern Italy. Garibaldi shook the king's hand and greeted him as the King of Italy. Even though he always dreamed of Italy being a republic, its unification was more important. Garibaldi refused to accept any honors, titles, decorations, or rewards for his role in the unification of Italy. As always, he wanted to remain independent.

Garibaldi and Victor Emmanuel on the bridge in Teano

The famous French writer, author of the *Three Musketeers*, Alexander Dumas, was dying to meet Garibaldi. He arrived on his yacht in Sicily. To his surprise, Garibaldi lived so modestly and had so little money that there were holes in his clothes, and he couldn't offer any fancy entertainment to his guests. "If I were rich like you," Garibaldi told Dumas apologetically, "I'd also get myself a yacht." Dumas was stunned, because soon after this conversation he saw Garibaldi sign a check for half a million francs... Garibaldi managed a lot of government money budgeted for his army, but he paid himself, the commander, only 10 francs a day.

After the war, Garibaldi retired to his farm on the island of Caprera. When the American Civil War began, Garibaldi expressed support for the Union. In 1861 he was approached by a US diplomat on behalf of President Lincoln. What would it take for Garibaldi to join the Union forces as a general, the diplomat inquired. Garibaldi said he would only agree to the role of the commander-in-chief, and only if slavery were to be abolished right away. Lincoln was not ready to abolish slavery immediately, so Garibaldi stayed in Italy.

Like most revolutionaries, Garibaldi was extremely anti-Catholic. To him the rule of the pope over the Papal States was just another monarchy. Garibaldi considered becoming a Protestant, but eventually he rejected Christianity altogether, proclaiming himself a deist – a person who discovers God by observing His creation, nature, rather than through the holy books and church tradition. In 1862 Garibaldi started gathering volunteers for a campaign against the Papal States under the slogan "Roma o Morte" (Rome or Death). With 2000 supporters he marched on Rome, but the army of Victor Emmanuel II stopped him. Garibaldi was wounded and kept as a prisoner until he recovered. The next time Garibaldi called together his volunteers was in 1866. With an army of 40,000 he participated in the Prussian war against Austria. The main victories, however, were won by the Prussians, so Garibaldi directed his troops – again – against Rome. But the pope's soldiers were better trained and equipped than Garibaldi's volunteers. He was wounded again, and, again, imprisoned for a short time.

Garibaldi's dream of the Papal States' defeat came true in 1870. During the Franco-Prussian War, the French garrison was removed from Rome. The pope was asked to abdicate (give up power) as the head of the Papal States. He refused. The Italian army laid siege to Rome and bombarded it from cannons for 3 hours until it surrendered. Rome became the capital of Italy, and Italy became a single nation, for the first time since the days of Ancient Rome. Garibaldi didn't participate in that campaign. He was in Caprera under an unofficial house arrest. Garibaldi wrote to his son-in-law: "My dear son, this garbage that calls itself the Italian government keeps me a prisoner in Caprera. I am here against my will, being watched day and night."

In 1875 Garibaldi was elected to the Italian parliament, and the government of the unified Italy sent him offers of government positions, titles and honors. Predictably, Garibaldi – again – declined to accept anything. He died in 1882, in Caprera, at the age of 75.

Left: Italian Wars of Independence commemorative medal

Right: Garibaldi fighting in Sicily
Below: Garibaldi on the way to the Battle of Mentana (against the troops of the Papal States)

KARL MARX
1818 – 1883

Karl Marx was a political theorist and an economist best known for creating the theory of socialist revolution and the *Marxist* economic theory explaining why – from the Marxist point of view – the *capitalist* economic and political system should be replaced with the *socialist* system.

Karl Marx was born in Germany. His dad, Heinrich Marx, was a lawyer and owner of vineyards. The family was Jewish, but Heinrich was a fan of Voltaire and had a negative attitude toward religion. To improve his career prospects, he and his wife converted to Christianity, but never practiced it. Karl Marx was home-schooled until he was 12. Then he went to a school where the principal was an acquaintance of his dad, a political liberal, who supported revolutionary-minded friends by employing them at his school as teachers. Some parents complained about the revolutionary and anti-Christian literature being distributed to the students. The police raided the school and many teachers were fired. At university, Marx studied law and economics... supposedly. Actually he spent time partying with his friends and running up huge debts. He also had a hot temper and was wounded in a duel. Heinrich Marx was horrified. He agreed to pay Karl's debts, but moved him to a different university that was more conservative. Soon Marx married Jenny von Westphalen, his childhood friend, who came from a family of German nobility.

Marx's political thinking started forming under the influence of the German philosopher Hegel. Hegel viewed the course of history as a spiral, where humanity returns to the same place with every new circle, but every time at a higher level. Heigel applied the idea of this spiral development to everything – the origins of the spiritual and material world, the development of knowledge and human society. Any process, according to Hegel, is the *dialectics* – logical progression from *thesis* (idea) to *antithesis* (its opposite) to *synthesis* (their combination). The opposites – thesis and antithesis – can't exist without each other. Light is not light if there is no 'non-light,' or darkness. A war is a war only if it is opposed to peace. The opposites 'struggle' with each other, achieving a new quality or result in the course of their interaction.

A slave is only a slave if he has a master. The master is not a master without a slave. Slavery is sustained by wars, and interrupted by slave uprisings, so the interaction between slaves and masters pushes political history forward. This view of reality and history became known as ***Hegel's dialectics*** or the ***dialectical method*** of interpreting reality. Marx applied it to the study of social forces, such as the working class and the 'capitalists' (business owners) whose struggle, Marx hoped, would lead to socialist revolution.

Hegel's thinking was rooted in Christian philosophy. For him, the material world was the result of a process that started on a spiritual level, as God's creation. This recognition of the spiritual world as the origin of the matter made Hegel's philosophy *idealistic*. Idea materializes and becomes a physical object or phenomenon. Karl Marx liked Hegel's 'dialectical method,' but rejected the spiritual, 'idealistic' aspects of Hegel's philosophy. In 1837 Marx met German anthropologist and philosopher Ludwig Feuerbach who tweaked Hegel's teaching into a system of thinking about the world as being entirely *material* and physical. He denied the existence of anything spiritual, attributing the spiritual to human imagination. Marx combined Hegel's and Feuerbach's ideas into what he called *dialectical materialism*. Feuerbach's words, "The philosophers have only interpreted the world in various ways. The point, however, is to change it," directed Marx to his lifetime goal – working out a roadmap to the socialist revolution.

As a university student Karl Marx was not sure what to do in terms of his future career. His dad wanted him to be a lawyer, but when Marx was 20, his dad died, and Marx tried to make a living as a writer. He wrote a novel, a play, and a series of poems, but soon gave up writing and switched to studying art history and translating ancient Roman literature from Latin into German. He completed his doctoral degree, but a career as a university professor was unlikely, because universities were mostly conservative. So Marx became a journalist, writing for a liberal newspaper. In 1843 the paper published an article making fun of the Russian monarchy. When the Russian Tsar Nicholas I heard of it, he demanded that the Prussian government ban the newspaper, and it was shut down.

The following year Marx met German socialist Friedrich Engels who became his lifelong collaborator. Engels suggested that it's the industrial workers (the ***working class***, or the ***proletariat***) that could propel a true socialist revolution. Marx and Engels focused on a transition from capitalism to socialism through a 'revolutionary proletarian movement' and a 'proletarian revolution.' The enemy of the proletariat is the **bourgeoisie** (the business owners, the capitalists), taught Marx and Engels. The capitalists own the **means of production** (plants, factories, businesses) and *exploit* the labor of the proletariat, paying workers very little. Therefore, a revolution is needed to take the 'means of production' from the capitalists and transfer those means to the workers, to save them from exploitation.

Capitalism

Capitalism is a political and economic system where 'capitalists' own the 'means of production' (shops, factories, companies). It's their **private property**. *Workers receive wages, but don't own the 'means of production' and the products they produce. You are free to start your own business using your own* **capital** *= money. When you sell products, the pricing is up to you. Workers that are more productive receive higher wages. There is equality of opportunity (anybody can start their own business or become more productive as a worker), but no equity (equality of outcome = equal income no matter whether you work hard or not). Most countries in the world have a capitalist economic system.*

Socialism

Socialism is a political and economic system where the 'means of production' (shops, factories, companies) are not private property, but the property of society as a whole. The state, on behalf of all the workers, owns all businesses and everything they produce. Workers receive wages and also benefits paid from the sales of the products they produce. The benefits include free housing, education, medical care, pensions and so on. However, under socialism, you can't start your own business, since all businesses belong to the state and all prices are determined by the government. There is equality of opportunity, plus equity (everybody has the same income, whether their work is good or bad).

The first country to try socialism was Russia, or, rather, the Soviet Union (or the USSR – Union of Soviet Socialist Republics) a socialist state formed on the territory of Russia after the revolution of 1917. The socialist system in the USSR lasted until 1989. It failed because of equity (equality of outcome): Workers had no motivation to become more productive or introduce innovation. In 1991 the Soviet Union fell apart, and its portions – Russia and 15 other 'socialist republics' – emerged as capitalist democracies, similar to traditionally-capitalist Western states.

The hammer and sickle – symbol of the socialist movement – represents the unity of industrial and agricultural workers; "The Worker and the Farmer" Soviet-era monument in Moscow, Russia.

Communism vs Socialism

The difference between Socialism and Communism according to Marx:
Socialism: "From each according to his ability, to each according to his work."
Communism: "From each according to his ability, to each according to his needs."

Under the socialist system people get paid for their work. And everyone is paid equally whether you are a talented, motivated and productive worker, or a lazy worker who doesn't produce much. Under this system people are not motivated to do their best at work, and the economy of socialism sooner or later falls apart – as happened in the Soviet Union.
Under the communist system people are supposed to get paid – equally – whether they work or not! Clearly, this system would deprive most workers of the motivation to work at all. That's why a communist system has never existed in real life.

Soviet

Since the Soviet Union (or 'Soviet Russia') was the first 'socialist' country, sometimes the word 'Soviet' is thought of as a synonym of 'socialist.' Actually 'Soviet' is a corruption of the Russian word *совет* (sah-vet) – 'council.' It refers to the system of local, regional, and federal councils that formed the government of the Soviet Union. A better translation of the 'Soviet Union' is the 'Union of Councils.'

A Russian soldier raises the flag of the Soviet Union over the Reichstag in Berlin in 1945, marking the victory of the Soviet Union over Nazi Germany.

In the 18th and 19th centuries most revolutionary movements were driven by various secret societies, such as Freemasons, Illuminati, Carbonari, and others. The majority of their members belonged to the 'educated' classes – university students, professors, noblemen, and politicians. Most of their work was done 'underground' – in total secrecy. Marx was a member of a couple secret revolutionary cells, but he believed that these secret societies were not enough to drive the 'proletarian revolution.' He wanted to create an organization similar to a political party that would unify the industrial workers of Europe against the bourgeoisie. As an attempt to create a workers' organization, Marx and Engels founded the Communist League and wrote their most popular joint work, the *Communist Manifesto*. The Manifesto opened with these famous words: "A ghost is haunting Europe – the ghost of communism." Most politicians had no idea what communism was, explained Marx and Engels. They labeled anyone who opposed them as 'communists,' and were unaware of the fact that the real-life communist movement was growing right under their nose.

The main points of the Communist Manifesto:

*The history of human society is the history of **class struggle** – the struggle of the working classes (slaves, industrial workers, peasants) against the classes that own the 'means of production' (capitalists, business owners).*

Sooner or later the proletariat – the industrial workers – would become aware of their power to change the society. They will unify within the communist movement, and socialist revolutions will sweep the world.

These socialist revolutions will then abolish private property and inheritance, bring all means of production under the control of the socialist state and create a 'classless' society – where everyone will work and there will be no wealthy classes exploiting the labor of the workers.

The famous last lines of the Communist Manifesto read, "Let the ruling classes tremble at a communist revolution. The proletarians have nothing to lose but their chains. They have a world to win. Workers of the world, unite!"

During the European revolutions of 1848, Marx published a revolutionary newspaper in Germany. A few times he was accused of anti-government activities and faced trial, but every time was acquitted. Finally, in 1849, Prussian authorities expelled him from the country, and Marx moved to London. To make some money, Marx worked as a foreign correspondent of the New York Daily Tribune. He also started working on his book *Das Kapital* (Capital) – his theory of marxist economics.

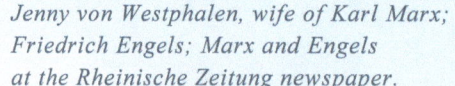

Jenny von Westphalen, wife of Karl Marx; Friedrich Engels; Marx and Engels at the Rheinische Zeitung newspaper.

While Marx and Engels were organizing the international communist movement, the sources of their own income were, ironically, fortunes made by 'capitalists' exploiting the 'proletariat.' Engels, who supported Marx financially, was a son of a wealthy industrialist. He inherited cotton spinning factories in England. English socialist James Guillaume described Engels as "a rich manufacturer accustomed to regard workmen as machine fodder and cannon fodder" (fodder = 'food, material'; 'machine fodder' = material used to run the machines; 'cannon fodder' = soldiers, 'food for cannons'). The other sources of Marx's income were the inheritance Marx received from his dad, and loans from the Philips family, Marx's rich uncle and cousins – the founders of *Philips Electronics*. Still, Marx's family could hardly make ends meet. They were deeply in debt and had to pawn the family's valuables and furniture. It didn't help that Marx was a heavy drinker, heavy smoker, worked almost exclusively at night, and took narcotics to battle insomnia. Karl Marx and Jenny had 7 kids, but because of poverty and disease only 3 of them lived to adulthood.

As if all that wasn't enough, the Marx family was shaken by a scandal. Karl Marx wasn't faithful to his wife, and had a baby with their housekeeper, Helen. Helen shared Marx's socialist views and worked for his family mostly for free – since he didn't have money to pay her. Her baby boy was given up for adoption, and only after Marx's death, his youngest daughter found her brother and made friends with him.

Pawnshop

A pawn shop is a business that loans money. People borrow money from a pawn shop by bringing in valuable items, such as jewelry, which they leave at the pawn shop until the loan is repaid. If the borrower fails to pay back the loan, their valuables are sold.

In 1864 Marx joined the *First International*, an organization that assembled members of many revolutionary secret societies. Its spirit was radically anti-government, anti-religion, anti-traditional-culture. Garibaldi visited one of the International's meetings and suggested that maybe it should encourage "faith in God." This statement was met with dead silence and raised eyebrows. Garibaldi panicked and explained that by "faith in God" he meant the worship of Reason, like in the days of the French Revolution.

At the First International, Marx clashed with the Russian anarchist and revolutionary Michael Bakunin. In their power struggle (which their critics called the 'spiders in a jar') Bakunin lost.

His writings are the source of the most biting criticism of Marx's personality. For example, "Marx's vanity . . . has no bounds," wrote Bakunin. "He is very jealous, very touchy, and very vindictive...Marx has never turned away from lies, no matter how mean they might be, if he could use them against those who had the misfortune to cause his anger." Bakunin predicted that if revolutionaries following Marx' teachings came to power, they would end up oppressing the working class rather than saving it from 'exploitation.' This prediction came true in totalitarian regimes, such as the Soviet Union, that attempted to build socialism following Marx's model.

In 1869 the International adopted the program outlined in the Communist Manifesto, including the abolition of private property and inheritance, and the trajectory toward worldwide revolution. Many noticed that the action points of this program coincided with those proposed by Adam Weishaupt, the founder of the 18th-century Bavarian secret society *Illuminati*. The critics of the communist movement accused Marx and his followers of being the tools of a destructive conspiracy, but the communists couldn't care less. Any influence that helped undermine social foundations, stir 'class hatred,' and make way for the revolution was welcome.

Totalitarianism

A totalitarian regime, or 'totalitarianism' is a political system that doesn't tolerate any opposition to the government, prohibits opposition parties, and punishes individuals and groups that protest against government policies. A totalitarian political system can exist in countries with either socialist or capitalist economic systems.

Marx died in 1883 in London. After his death Engels became critical of the idea of a violent worldwide revolution he and Marx had promoted, and suggested that perhaps there was "a peaceful, democratic road to socialism."

Many believe that the triangular 'Eye of the Providence' on the Great Seal of the United States (and on the $1 bill) is a symbol of the Illuminati. Indeed, in the 18th century it was used as a masonic symbol, but prior to that it appeared in Christian art symbolizing the Trinity.

Illuminati

Illuminati was a secret society founded in 1776 in Bavaria by a German professor of Canon Law (church law), Adam Weishaupt. Illuminati is the plural of the Latin adjective 'illuminatus' = 'enlightened.' The society focused on spreading the political ideas of Voltaire and other philosophers of the Enlightenment, and anti-Christian doctrines. Illuminati adopted the ideas of worldwide revolution, abolition of private property and inheritance, and the justification of violence committed to achieve revolutionary goals ("The end justifies the means"). They also called to destroy all social ties in the society, such as marriage, family, and patriotism to "make the human race one good and happy family." The Illuminati were banned in Bavaria and dispersed into other secret societies and masonic lodges.

CECIL RHODES
1853 – 1902

In 1869-70, after diamonds were discovered in South Africa, thousands of adventurers from Europe came there in search of riches. Sailors ran away from their ships, soldiers deserted from the army, settlers left their farms, and shop owners sold their stores to test their luck in the 'diamond rush.' Along with them came an 18-year-old Englishman, Cecil Rhodes. The trip from London to South Africa took over 2 months in those days. Cecil didn't seek fortune. He was sick with tuberculosis and his doctor said he had no more than a year to live, so his dad sent him to South Africa where, he hoped, the dry air would heal his son. Cecil ended up in the town of Kimberley in the British Cape colony, working in diamond mines. He arrived in Kimberley in an ox-driven cart, carrying with him a bucket and a spade, several volumes of classical Latin and Greek literature, and a dictionary of Ancient Greek.

When Cecil Rhodes saved enough money, he bought his own *claim*. A mining claim is an area of land where the mine owner has purchased the right to extract mineral deposits. When Rhodes became a claim owner, he continued working side-by-side with his native African miners. They pulled ropes, lifting buckets of blue clay from the depth of the mines. A blue color in the clay signaled the presence of Kimberlite, diamond-bearing igneous rock named after the town of Kimberley where it was first identified.

Kimberley diamond mine, 19th century;
Right: Descending into Kimberley mine

The larger kimberlite rocks were crushed into pieces and Cecil inspected every bit looking for diamonds. He also tried other businesses – selling ice to the miners, and pumping water out of mines with the help of an old engine he had repaired. Soon he was making good money. But wealth didn't excite Cecil Rhodes. His dream was to unify all the lands and colonies in South and Central Africa under British rule.

Rhodes traveled back to England to study at Oxford University. His health improved, and he loved telling his friends how, once back in England, he visited his doctor. The doctor said, "You the same Rhodes? According to my books, you have been in your grave for some time! Here is the entry: Tuberculosis. Recovery impossible." At Oxford Rhodes joined a masonic lodge. However, he came to the conclusion that masons lacked unity and 'big ideas' to help him fulfill his dream of colonizing Africa. Rhodes considered creating his own secret society to bring the entire world under British rule. In his 1877 essay *Confession of Faith* he wrote: "Africa is still lying ready for us. It is our duty to take it. It is our duty to seize every opportunity of acquiring more territory and we should keep this one idea steadily before our eyes that more territory simply means more of the Anglo-Saxon race, more of the best, the most human, most honorable race the world possesses."

Meanwhile, the 'diamond boom' put so many gems on the market that their prices started crashing, bringing an end to 'diamond fever.' The shares of mining companies were getting cheaper, many **randlords** (mining claim owners) were eager to 'cash out' – sell their business. That's when Cecil Rhodes decided to start buying smaller diamond mines. His plan was to create a diamond **monopoly** and limit the output of the mines and the quantities of diamonds on the market to keep the price of diamonds as high as possible. To achieve this, he asked the Rothschild banking family for a massive loan. The Rothschilds were stunned, given the fact that Rhodes was just a kid in his early 20s. The answer was, "Give us a few days to think this over." To that Rhodes responded, "My time is valuable. I will see you in an hour. If you haven't decided by that time, I'll seek assistance elsewhere."

An hour later he had his loan. Within the next 17 years Cecil Rhodes bought practically all the mines in the Kimberley area, becoming the biggest of the 'randlords.'

> ### *Monopoly*
> If a company is the only supplier of a particular product, it has a 'monopoly' on this product. Monopoly is the control of supply with no competition.

Diamond mine workers' compound

One of the mines in which Rhodes invested was called "the old De Beers" after the name of the Boer farmers that owned the land around the mine. In 1888, with the investment from the Rothschilds, Rhodes founded **De Beers Consolidated Mines** that would become De Beers, the biggest diamond supplier in the world. Africans who worked for De Beers had to live in special guarded compounds on the territory of the mines. They were searched before and after work and fed only bread with salt (which resulted in scurvy, a disease caused by a lack of vitamin C). White workers were trusted. They were free from searches and could live at home in colonial towns.

In 1880, Rhodes got involved in politics in the Cape colony, was elected to its parliament, and ten years later became its prime minister. In politics he didn't hesitate to do favors, buy votes, and pay journalists to praise him. "Find the man's price," was his formula. To bring under his influence a potential political enemy, Rhodes offered to pay for his trip to Europe... when a local tribe agreed with his policies, Rhodes donated enough money to them to buy a thousand-acre farm... He charmed his supporters with a *populist* stance. Despite his wealth, he always wore the same old hat...when visiting settlers' villages he was dressed in a cheap old suit, ate canned beef and crackers his company served to workers and police for dinner, and slept in a native hut.

Rhodes' view of native Africans was typically colonial. He believed they were lazy 'savages,' and, as a prime minister, he pushed through the laws that drove them from their lands.

His goal, of course, was to clear the way for mining and industrial development, but he justified his position by saying that getting Africans off the land "stimulates" them to work. "The natives are like children," he wrote. "They are just emerging from barbarism."

Cecil Rhodes consistently pursued his idea of adding more and more African lands to the British Empire. His method was to purchase mining rights from African tribal chiefs. Once the mining rights were granted by these local rulers, the areas were made British **protectorates** – areas 'protected' by defense agreements with the British Empire, which effectively made them British colonies. The defense treaties allowed Rhodes to convince other investors and developers to bring their business to the new territories since they were considered 'safe.' In 1889 Rhodes created the *South Africa Company* (modeled after the East India Company) and received from the British government a *charter* (permit, agreement) that allowed it to govern, police, and make new treaties with the native tribes from South Africa all the way to Central Africa.

> ### *Populism*
>
> *Populism is a political narrative that contrasts the 'people' (workers, common citizens, voters) against the supposedly corrupt and self-serving 'elites.' The elites may include the wealthy and powerful interest groups that control the media and manipulate elections, professors who are paid to brainwash college students, the 'deep state' government cliques that betray people's interests, and so on. Populist politicians criticize the elites and try to look and behave like their voters, the common citizens.*

Looking for gold, hundreds of British colonists launched expeditions toward Central Africa. They were accompanied by heavily armed police hired by the South Africa Company. Most areas were roadless. At every step explorers had to cut their way through dense bush. At night *Maxim machine guns* (the first fully automatic gun invented in 1884) were placed at the corners of each camp and an electric light was used to scare away native people. The territories where Cecil Rhodes' company operated were named after him – *Southern Rhodesia* (modern Zimbabwe), *North-Eastern Rhodesia* and *North-Western Rhodesia* (modern Zambia).
These territories were eventually annexed by Britain and became British colonies.

The Maxim gun

Local tribes often rebelled because Rhodes paid his police, soldiers, and managers with land that belonged to the native people. As a result, the South Africa Company fought wars against the native tribes. In 1893, Rhodes' troops fought the *First Matabele War* against the African *Ndebele* kingdom in modern-day Zimbabwe. As a result of their using the Maxim machine gun, about 10 thousand Ndebele were killed. Only about 100 British soldiers perished. Over a thousand large farms were founded and given to white settlers and soldiers on the Ndebele land. Lobengula, the king of the Ndebele tribes, called Cecil Rhodes a "brother who eats whole countries for his dinner." After the war the South Africa Company demanded from Lobengula 1000 head of cattle as indemnity (compensation) for war expenses, and gave the cattle to its troops as a reward. The company also started organizing regular cattle- and corn-looting raids on Ndebele villages. It even had a special department called the Loot Committee!

After the war hundreds of Ndebele began dying of smallpox and starvation. The British prevented them from sowing their crops until they surrendered their weapons. Cecil Rhodes' friend and a famous lion hunter, Frederick Selous, who fought in the Matabele Wars, wrote in his memoir: "Short of food, and living like wild beasts in the rocks and forests, with all the bitter discomfort which such a life entails even on savages during the rainy season in a sub-tropical country, they saw their women and children get sick and die, day by day."

The British wars in Africa were summed up in these sarcastic lines by the British writer Hilaire Belloc in 1898 ('The Modern Traveler'):
 "Whatever happens, we have got,
  The Maxim Gun, and they have not."

Ndebele warriors, South Africa Company advertising, and a vintage photo "Starting for Matabele War, Oct. 7th, 1893"

In 1894 Rhodes visited Mpondoland where local tribes were on the verge of a riot as their land was being taken over by the South Africa Company. He ordered one of his soldiers to flatten a field of corn with machine gun fire and informed the Mpondo tribesmen that they would be burned just like that if they dared to rebel.

Rhodes viewed Boers in the same way as he viewed native Africans – as a lower grade of human. He was angry with the government of the gold-rich Boer Republic of the Transvaal for not cooperating with the British in matters important for the mining industries. So in 1895 Rhodes ordered British officer Leander Starr Jameson to invade Transvaal with a small military force and attempt to overthrow the Transvaal government. The invasion, known as the **Jameson Raid**, ended up in a disaster, with a few dozen British soldiers killed. It eventually led to the **Second Boer War** between the Boers of Transvaal and the British that took tens of thousands of lives. As a result of the Jameson Raid, Rhodes had to resign as the Cape colony prime minister.

Soon after the Jameson Raid, the native tribes of **Ndebele** and **Shona** acquired firearms, rebelled again, and attacked settlers on the territory controlled by the South Africa Company. Among the casualties were white women and kids. While native Africans viewed any member of an enemy tribe as a target, including women and children, the white settlers saw such attacks as savagery and this made it easy for Rhodes to justify a ruthless campaign against the Africans.

Boer troops

Rhodes personally led his police and troops to suppress the rebellion, instructing his soldiers to "do the most harm you can to the natives." He was also quoted saying, "You should kill all you can. It serves as a lesson to them when they talk things over at night. And they begin to fear you.' Selous described one of the raids he led: "We fired on the tribesmen at sight, and although they offered no resistance, but ran away as hard as they could, we chased them and kept on firing at them as long as we could see them." Here is how Selous' described the aftermath of 'punishing' retreating native tribesmen: "A long line of corpses marked the track where the whirlwind of the white man's vengeance had swept along. *Vae victis*!" (Latin for "Woe to the defeated!") Shona and Ndebele, however, also fought between themselves. When the Shona cattle thieves stole some of the Ndebele's cattle, the Ndebele killed 400 Shona in one raid. Lack of unity made Africans especially vulnerable. Rhodes used the clashes between the native tribes to justify his policies, claiming that the British were 'saving' the Shona from the Ndebele.

Up to 10,000 Ndebele and Shona, and 372 white settlers were killed in this new war. And the native uprisings didn't stop. At some point the British government started asking questions about Rhodes' activity in Africa. They instructed the British Colonial Secretary to call Rhodes to London to explain the British defeat in the Jameson Raid. Rhodes came armed with documents proving that the Colonial Secretary had been informed about the raid before it started. Rhodes used this to blackmail the Secretary and other British government bureaucrats and they left him alone. Meanwhile the South Africa Company adopted a ***scorched earth strategy*** against the rebellious African tribes, burning their villages, fields, and grain stores, and blowing up their caves and shelters at the slightest suspicion of rebellion. An 1897 British military intelligence officer's report read: "It seems to me that the only way of doing anything at all with these natives is to starve them, destroy their lands, and kill all that can be killed."

The 'Scorched Earth' Strategy

Scorched Earth is a military strategy of completely destroying enemy infrastructure – buildings, roads, bridges, power, food, water supplies – anything that allows the enemy to survive and fight a war.

Cecil Rhodes never married, had no kids, and was rumored to be a hater of women. The only woman who claimed he was interested in her was Princess Catherine Radziwill, a Polish noblewoman from Russia (Poland was a province of the Russian Empire between 1795 and 1917). Radziwill was an adventurer and a con artist. Married to a German prince, she lived at the German imperial court, but was banished from Germany for anonymously publishing

Princess Catherine Radziwill

gossip about the German royal family. She moved back to Russia, but soon abandoned her husband and 5 kids and was off for adventures in Europe and Africa. She met Rhodes on a steamboat, on her way to South Africa, and Rhodes invited her to a party at his estate. He knew right away that was a huge mistake. The princess decided to marry Rhodes and followed him everywhere, spreading rumors that he was in love with her. Rhodes paid her hotel bill on the condition that she would leave South Africa, but the princess was not easy to get rid of. Next she claimed she and Rhodes had a baby and demanded that he marry her! (Actually the baby's dad was Rhodes' building contractor associate.)

Finally Rhodes left for London, relieved that he and Radziwill were – for a change – not on the same continent. But the princess used his absence productively. She forged his signature on documents stating that he owed her money, waved them at a bank and borrowed cash to pay her debts. Once back in South Africa, Rhodes was able to prove that his signature was a fake, and sued Radziwill. Radziwill tried to blackmail him, hinting that she had some secret documents Rhodes didn't want to have published. At that point Cecil Rhodes was very sick and let go of the court case until Radziwill suddenly sued him back, demanding money based on the papers she forged. The court proceedings restarted, but Cecil Rhodes died before the final hearing of the case, in 1902. His last words were, "So little done, so much to do." Radziwill was sentenced to two years in jail for forgery. After she served her term, she started writing a book – *Cecil Rhodes: Man and Empire Maker*. And there were more adventures ahead: In 1913 Radziwill published gossip about the Russian royal family and was kicked out of Russia. She ended up in New York City where she lived until her death in 1941.

One of the best-known parts of Cecil Rhodes legacy is the **Rhodes Scholarships** program that pays for 83 postgraduate students to study each year at Oxford University in England. In the 1880s new colleges and universities were founded in many British colonies and territories. The 'traveling scholarships' became popular as a way of bringing British educational standards and academic culture to these new schools. Rhodes viewed such programs as an important empire-building tool, necessary to strengthen British culture and the imperial ideology in the colonies. The Rhodes Scholarships were created after Cecil Rhodes death, based on his will.

De Beers 50-100 Years Later...

To sell as many diamonds as they could, at the highest possible price, the De Beers company had to control not only the supply of diamonds (which they controlled with a monopoly on diamond extraction), but also the demand for diamonds! How to make people want diamonds? How to persuade even those who had no interest in jewelry and couldn't afford luxury items to buy a diamond?... And, once someone has acquired a diamond, how to prevent them from reselling it? De Beers made this happen. Can you guess how?...

In 1938 De Beers hired a Philadelphia ad agency, N.W. Ayer & Son, to change 'the image' of a diamond as a luxury item for the wealthy. N.W. Ayer proposed to link diamonds to something 'emotional'... to something in every person's life...That's how the 'tradition' of a diamond engagement ring as a token of love and loyalty was born. Yes, it's a fake 'tradition' invented to create the demand for diamonds. Engagement rings existed since the times of Ancient Rome, but they came with various gems and were not an obligatory part of the engagement ritual. Diamonds had not been associated with marriage until De Beers.

"Create a situation where almost every person pledging marriage feels compelled to acquire a diamond engagement ring" – that's how N.W. Ayer's formulated their plan. In 1947 Frances Gerety, a copy writer for N.W. Ayer, wrote the famous 'signature line' for De Beers advertising campaigns, "A diamond is forever." Initially De Beers ad campaigns put pressure on men to spend one month's salary on a diamond engagement ring for their future bride. By the 1940s De Beers came up with: "Isn't two months' salary a small price to pay for something that lasts forever?" ...

In the 1960s, the Soviet Union began diamond mining in the Arctic regions of Russia. Russians were interested in diamonds for industrial use, not for jewelry, so they offered De Beers the right to buy all of Russia's excess diamonds – if De Beers still wanted to preserve their diamond monopoly. De Beers agreed. But shortly after, Russian diamond mining technology improved to such an extent that, along with large, jewelry-grade diamonds, De Beers was forced to buy huge quantities of small 'optical' diamonds coming out of Russia's mines. How to sell those small diamonds to people who had already bought engagement rings? Leave it to De Beers: They invented the Eternity Ring!
Around 2000 the De Beers monopoly was broken, and the Russian Alrosa company emerged as the world's #1 supplier of diamonds.

Vintage De Beers ad and the Eternity Ring

Heinrich Schliemann
1822 – 1890

Heinrich Schliemann was a German businessman and an archaeologist. He is best known for his excavations and discoveries on the site of ancient Troy, the city-state the Greek poet Homer described in his epic poems the *Iliad* and the *Odyssey*. In the 19th century most scholars agreed that Troy existed only in legend. Schliemann's dad, a Lutheran minister, read the *Iliad* and the *Odyssey* to his kids in German translations. And unlike grownups around him, Heinrich Schliemann believed that Troy was real, and that the stories of Homer's poems reflected actual historical events. Schliemann recalled that at the age of 7 he decided to become an archeologist and find Troy.

Schliemann's family was poor. Heinrich had 8 siblings. His mom died when he was 9, and when he was 11 his dad was accused of embezzling (stealing) church money, lost his job, and couldn't afford university education for his kids. At 14 Schliemann was hired as an apprentice (student-helper) at a bakery shop, and worked there for 5 years, until he was injured lifting heavy boxes. Then he found a job on a sailboat leaving for Latin America, but the ship got caught in a storm off the coast of the Netherlands and sank. Heinrich Schliemann ended up in Amsterdam, doing odd jobs to survive.

Eventually, when Heinrich was 22 he was hired by a Dutch trading company that sent him as their representative to St.Petersburg, Russia. This was Schliemann's big break. He started learning Russian and discovered that mastering foreign languages was one of his talents. He even came up with a system of language-learning and boasted that he could speak a foreign language after only 6 weeks of studies! By 24, in addition to his native German, he spoke French, Dutch, Italian, English, Spanish, Portuguese, Russian, and Greek. One of Heinrich's older brothers went to the United States and made a fortune during the 1840s 'gold rush' in California. He died in 1850, having left some of his fortune to Heinrich. Heinrich moved to Sacramento, California, speculated in gold dust (bought and resold it at a higher price) and even founded a bank. Two years later he sold his business and returned to Russia, where he married Catherine Lyzhina, the niece of a wealthy St. Petersburg businessman.

Schliemann continued doing business in Russia – very successfully – buying and reselling various goods, such as indigo dye, coffee, as well as gunpowder and ammunition for the Russian army during the Crimean War. In 1858, when Schliemann turned 36, he decided he was wealthy enough to retire and dedicate the rest of his life to searching for ancient Troy. "In the midst of the bustle of business I had never forgotten Troy, nor the promise I made to my father to excavate it," he wrote. He started visiting and studying ancient sites in Greece and the Ottoman Empire and published a book in which he promoted the idea that the ruins of Troy were located underneath the Turkish coastal town of Hisarlik. Hoping to win some academic credibility, Schliemann submitted this book as a doctoral dissertation to the University of Rostock in Germany and received his doctoral degree. His critics, however, claimed that his work consisted of translations from other authors, including Frank Calvert, a British diplomat and self-taught archaeologist who lived in Turkey and was one of the first to suggest that the *mound* (hill) in Hisarlik was the site of Troy.

Schliemann's wife, Catherine

In 1866 Schliemann decided to move from St.Petersburg to Paris where he was planning to speculate in real estate and study at the Sorbonne University. But his wife, Catherine, didn't like Europe, wanted her kids to grow up Russian Orthodox Christians, and refused to leave Russia. Schliemann threatened to divorce her, but she didn't care. Their relationship had already been wrecked: Schliemann spent so much time away from home traveling, that she assumed he had lost interest in her. Although divorce was permitted by the Russian Orthodox Church, it was rare and scandalous. Two years later, looking for an easier way to end his marriage, Schliemann moved to Indianapolis, Indiana, where the law allowed a divorce in the absence of the spouse being divorced. The *Indianapolis Daily Journal* wrote that the city was crowded with "divorce hunting men and women." Schliemann lied in court stating that he permanently lived in the US and planned to stay in Indiana. To support his claim, he bought a house in Indianapolis and shares in a local Indiana company.

While waiting for the court to grant him a divorce, Schliemann asked his friends to find him a Greek wife. He also published an ad in an Athens newspaper looking for a bride who could also be an archaeologist's assistant. He spoke fluent Greek and thought of moving permanently to Greece. "I find it impossible to live anywhere but on classical soil," he wrote.

Friends and strangers started sending Schliemann dozens of photographs of potential brides, praising their enthusiasm for Homer and archaeology. Schliemann selected the niece of a friend from Athens, 17-year-old Sophia Engastromenos. After the Indiana court finalized his divorce, Schliemann sold his Indianapolis house, left for Athens, and two months later he and Sophia were married. The couple had two kids named after Homer's characters – Andromache and Agamemnon. When the babies were baptized, Schliemann added his own touch to the ceremony by putting a book of *Iliad* on their heads and reading his favorite passages from Homer in ancient Greek.

In 1870 Schliemann started excavations in Turkey. The academic community disliked him, viewing him as a rich adventurer with no real education. But Frank Calvert didn't mind collaborating with Schliemann and invited him to dig on the land purchased by his wealthy brother in Hisarlik. Calvert had already spent 7 years excavating there. The Calverts ran a tour guide business in the area and owned a farm with a large residential compound where many archaeologists stayed while traveling in Turkey. In a secret room of the main house Frank Calvert kept his collection of archaeological finds. Schliemann had a huge budget. He hired 80 workers. Both he and his wife Sophia worked on the site from dawn to dusk along with their team. In winter the Schliemanns couldn't keep a lamp lit at night because icy winds blew through every crack in their small cottage. Their drinking water was frozen by the morning. "We had nothing to keep us warm except our enthusiasm for the great work of discovering Troy," wrote Schliemann. As they were digging up the Hissarlik mound, at 28-29 feet deep they found ancient vases, copper tools, shields and knives...

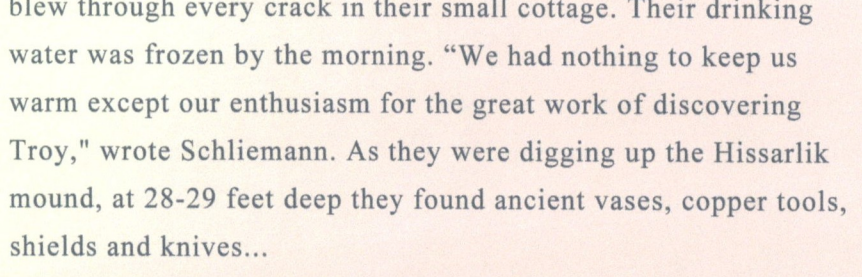

Sophia Schliemann and the Hisarlik mound ruins excavated by Henrich Schliemann

Gold jewelry from the 'Treasure of Priam' at the Pushkin Museum of Fine Arts in Moscow, Russia; Sophia Schliemann wearing a headdress, necklace, and earrings from the 'Treasure of Priam'

In June 1873, one day before they were supposed to leave, the workers' shovels hit a large copper vessel. Inside was a dazzling treasure of 9000 gold and silver objects – diadems, jewelry, belts, bracelets... Schliemann announced that he found the treasure of Priam, the last king of Troy, and the jewelry that belonged to the legendary beauty Helen of Troy. Many disbelieved and even suggested Schliemann 'planted' the artifacts on the site to fake a great discovery. This event, however, attracted dozens of archeologists to the site, and soon they found the ruins of nine cities buried one under another, spanning 3,600 years. Which one of them was Troy?...One layer was all ashes, so Schliemann thought that was the historical Troy, since, according to Homer, it was burned by the Greek armies. But later it became clear that the 'burned layer' was formed between 3,000 and 2,000 BC. It was much older than Homer's Troy.

Turkish authorities demanded half of the finds from Hisarlik. Schliemann gave up some artifacts, but smuggled the gold "treasure of Priam" out of the country into Greece.
The government of the Ottoman Empire sued him in Greek court. Schliemann paid a fine – five times more than what they demanded, and so he was left alone and given permission to continue digging. Looking for a 'home' for his treasures, Schliemann offered them to Greek, French, and Russian museums. But professional archaeologists and scholars, envious of Schliemann's success, declared his finds fake. Only in 1881 were his collections accepted by the Ethnographic Museum in Berlin.

"Priam's gold" was in Berlin until 1945. As the Soviet army defeated Hitler and occupied Berlin, the 3 crates of Schliemann's artifacts were flown to Moscow as compensation for the Russian art and cultural treasures stolen by the German army (many of which have never been found and returned). To avoid legal claims from post-war Germany, the transfer of Schliemann's gold to Moscow was kept secret. Only after the Soviet Union fell apart in 1991, did the Russian authorities extract "Priam's gold" from the basement of the Pushkin Museum in Moscow and put it on display.

In 1876 Schliemann began digging at Mycenae, Greece. He wanted to prove that one of the heroes of Homer's *Iliad*, King Agamemnon of Mycenae (the commander of the Greek armies during the Trojan War) was a real historical figure. Again, he was very fortunate. He discovered the so-called Shaft Graves, a 16th-century BC royal cemetery located at the gates of the ancient Mycenae fortress. From the graves they lifted well-preserved skeletons, pottery, jewelry, and gold masks, including the so-called 'Mask of Agamemnon.' Schliemann sent a telegram to the King of Greece saying he had found the tomb of Agamemnon. The Mask of Agamemnon, however, was later dated to 300 years prior to the possible start of the Trojan War.

The 'Mask of Agamemnon' (below), the Mycenae graves circle, and other treasures from Mycenae

Over the years scholars became more and more critical of Schliemann's work. It turned out, Schliemann's archaeological methods were rough and unprofessional, even by the standards of his era. For instance, he used dynamite to speed up the excavation process, destroying a lot of valuable archaeological data and artifacts. He kept hardly any records while digging – a mortal sin in archaeology! Digging through the layers of ruins under Hisarlik he, likely, forever destroyed the layer of the actual historical Troy. In archaeological literature angry scholars call Schliemann a 'vandal,' a 'pathological liar,' and a 'thief.' Indeed, some of Schliemann's discoveries were proven to be fakes. In 1887-88 he 'planted' a few artifacts on a site in Alexandria where he hoped to look for the tomb of Alexander the Great. Then he 'discovered' them, which convinced the local authorities to give him a permit to dig. Modern scholars believe that the "Priam's gold" on display in Moscow was also artificially put together by Schliemann to make his discovery more impressive. Describing the moment the treasure was found, Schliemann wrote that he had dismissed his workers as soon as the gold sparkled from under the sand, dug it out with his wife Sophia, and smuggled it away in her scarf. Meanwhile, at the moment of discovery Sophia was away, in Athens, at her dad's funeral.

Despite all this, it's hard to deny Schliemann's contribution to archaeology. He made archaeology fashionable. That was, perhaps, his greatest achievement. The whole world followed his adventures and admired his discoveries. Every newspaper reported his finds and quoted his diaries. He was the original rock star of archeology, who inspired hundreds of young people to enter this exciting field.

'Lion Gate' in Mycenae; Home of Heinrich Schliemann, Athens

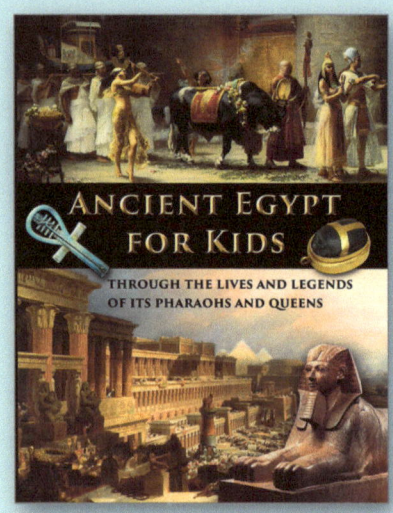
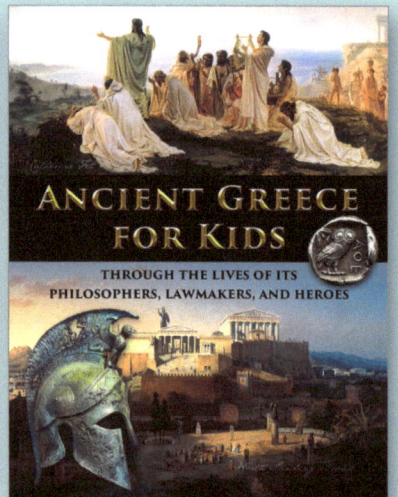
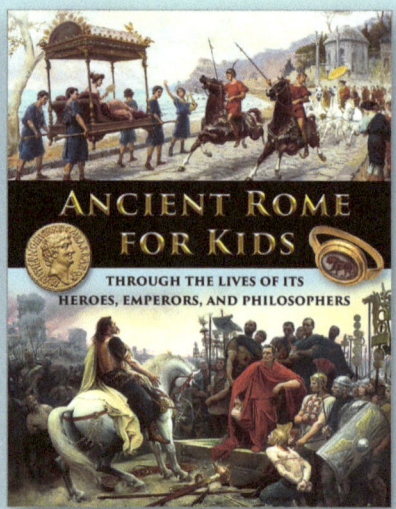
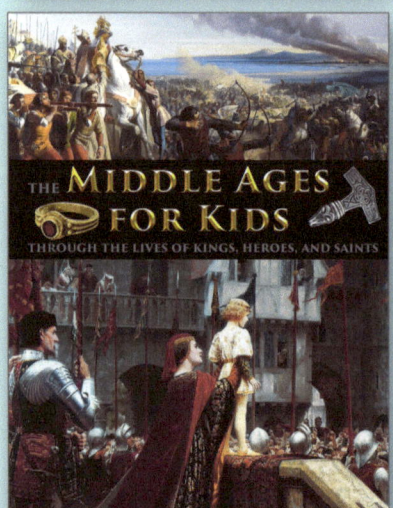
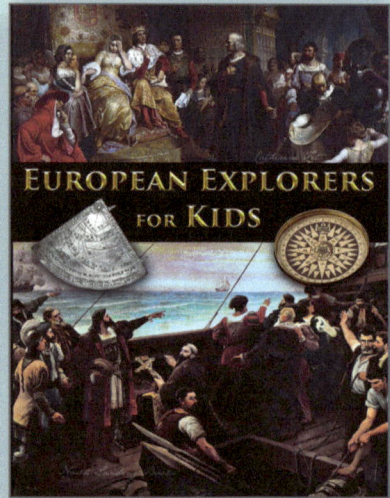
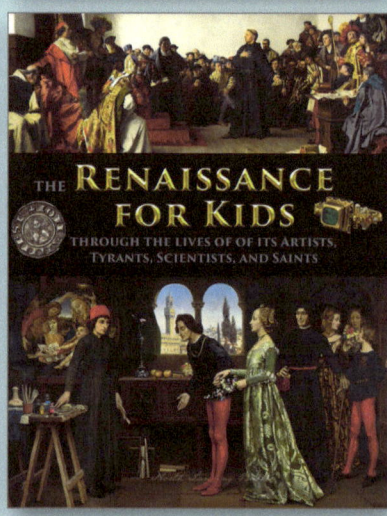
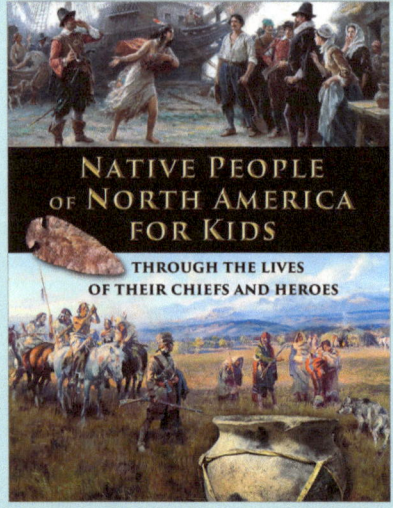
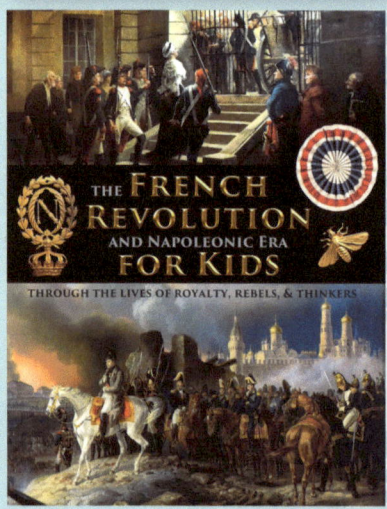
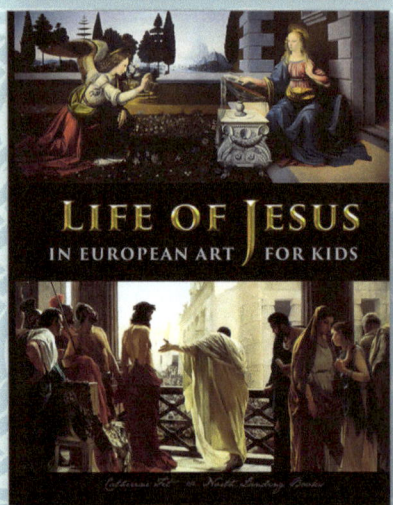

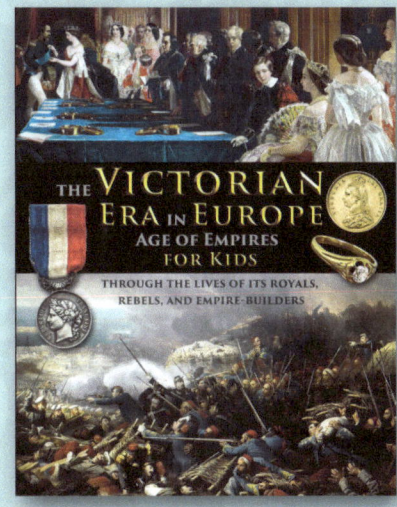
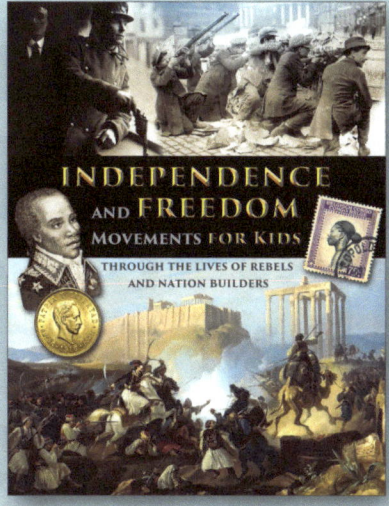
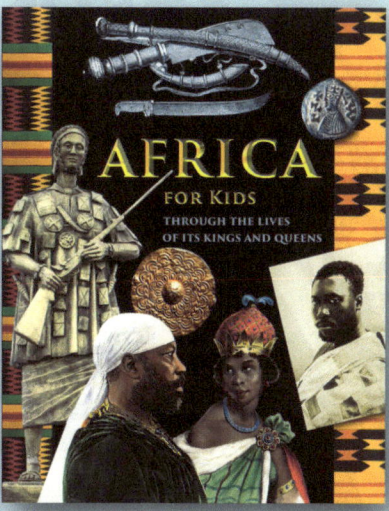
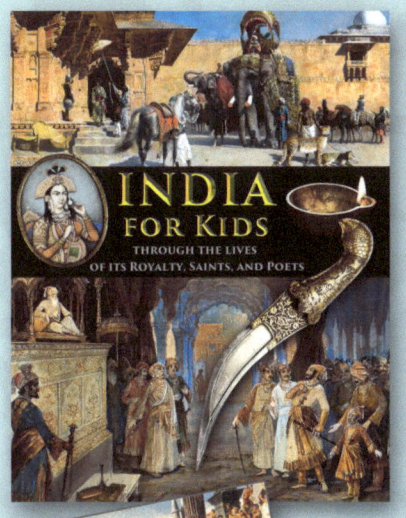
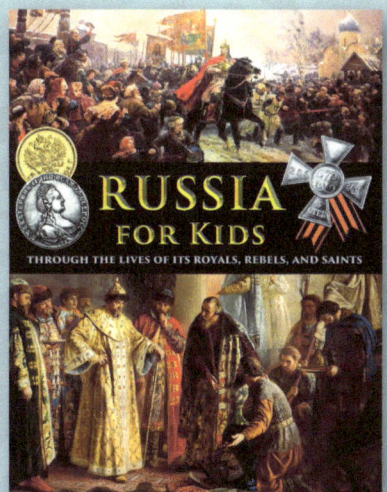

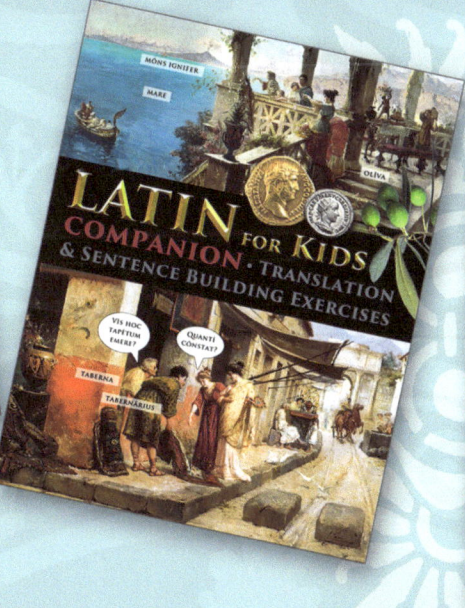
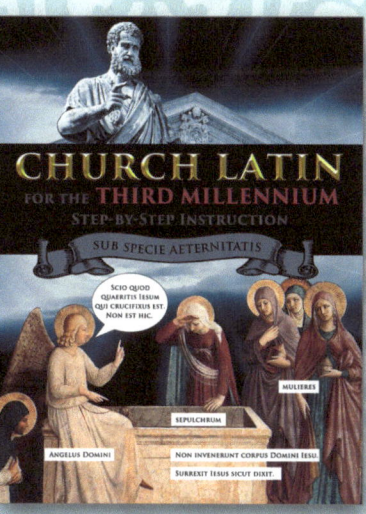

www.ingramcontent.com/pod-product-compliance
Lightning Source LLC
LaVergne TN
LVHW071657060526
838201LV00037B/367